FORGERY

For Phil, one of the "1817 Oak Street Boys," whose enduring friendship has made the load always lighter.

Acknowledgments

This book would not have become a reality without the loving support of my wife, Joan. Thanks to Joan Rainis, Caroline Rainis, Lori Miner, and Barb Clay for providing writing samples, and to Ann Rainis for graciously providing access to old family documents concerning my grandfather, William Rainis. Special thanks to Jim Hayes for help in procuring special Revolutionary War period and presidential documents. Thanks to Joe Elliot and Mathew Bacon of School Specialty, Inc., for their support. Special thanks to Ken Rando for helping with the electrons.

Library of Congress Cataloging-in-Publication Data

Rainis, Kenneth G.
    Forgery : crime-solving science experiments / Kenneth G. Rainis.
       p. cm. — (Forensic science projects)
    Includes bibliographical references and index.
    ISBN 0-7660-1961-6 (hardcover)
       1. Forgery—Juvenile literature.   2. Forgery—Case studies—Juvenile literature. 3. Forensic sciences—Juvenile literature. I. Title.
    HV6675.R35 2006
    363.25'963—dc22

                    2005029212

Printed in the United States of America

10 9 8 7 6 5 4 3 2 1

To Our Readers: We have done our best to make sure all Internet Addresses in this book were active and appropriate when we went to press. However, the author and the publisher have no control over and assume no liability for the material available on those Internet sites or on other Web sites they may link to. Any comments or suggestions can be sent by e-mail to comments@enslow.com or to the address on the back cover.

Illustration credits: All illustrations and photos by Kenneth G. Rainis, except as noted: © 2006 Jupiterimages Corporation, pp. 3, 8, 52, 62, 68; Copyright © From *Scientific Examination of Questioned Documents* by Ordway Hilton. Reproduced by permission of Routledge/Taylor & Francis Group, LLC, p. 81; © Corel Corporation, 20; Private collection, pp. 92, 99; Time Life Pictures, p. 6.

Background Photo credits: John Foxx / © 2001 Copyright ImageState; © SuperStock, Inc.(chapter opener image).

Cover Photo Credit: Copyright © Image Source Limited

FORENSIC SCIENCE PROJECTS

FORGERY

Crime-Solving Science Experiments

Kenneth G. Rainis

Science Consultant:
Jeffrey H. Luber
Diplomate, American Board of
Forensic Document Examiners

Enslow Publishers, Inc.
40 Industrial Road
Box 398
Berkeley Heights, NJ 07922
USA
http://www.enslow.com

CONTENTS

CHAPTER 1

The Case of the Document Changer

Mark Hofmann (1954–) was a well-known document dealer. He bought and sold historical records. He was also a forger—one of the best. He used paper and ink to make fake documents. He hoped to become rich by selling these phony items.

A forger is a type of actor. Like any great actor, Hofmann had to prepare for his performance. He had to become familiar with history and how it related to the document he was planning to forge. Hofmann needed

the correct materials with which to create his performance. He had to obtain the correct ink and paper to make a document that was believable. Hofmann had the unique ability to place himself in an almost trancelike state. This allowed him to imitate the rhythm and flow of a

Mark Hofmann was a well known document dealer. He was also a document forger.

person's handwriting. That was his secret to creating a believable handwritten line.

Expert forensic document examiners have linked Hofmann to the forgery of documents by over 129 individuals—more than any other forger. Among his many creations were historical Mormon forgeries.

Hofmann was brought up in the Mormon Church. He knew that Mormon Church officials would be very interested in viewing certain documents. Such interest would make Hofmann's newly created forged documents desirable and valuable. This was his chance to turn paper and ink into gold.

In 1981 Hofmann started work in his basement in Salt Lake City to create a counterfeit document—the Joseph III blessing. Hofmann intended to create this document to show that Joseph Smith (1805–1844), the founder of the Mormon Church, had given his blessing to his son, Joseph III, instead of to Brigham Young, to continue the work of the church. The modern Mormon Church believed that such a documented event would give the other, smaller branch of the Mormon Church— the Reorganized Church of Jesus Christ of Latter-day Saints—founded by his son, Joseph Smith III (1832–1914), legitimacy. To the main church, the document was an embarrassment, weakening Brigham Young's claim as its true leader. To the smaller branch of the church, the same document gave them true claim as heirs of the Mormon Church. Hofmann reasoned that the Mormon Church would pay a very high price to own—and hide—such a document.

First Hofmann needed paper from the early 1830s. He decided to use the unprinted pages from genuine books in the library of the Mormon college, Brigham Young University. He realized that old paper loses its surface finish and gradually becomes rough. Ink applied to old paper would spread out or "feather"—a sure sign of a forger's hand. Hofmann developed a special dipping technique. He coated the paper with gelatin so that the ink he applied would not feather. Next, he needed ink used in the 1830s. Unlike most forgers, he researched a formula and made his own.

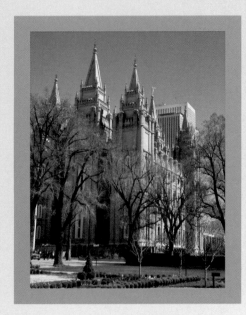

The Mormon church paid high prices for church documents, which turned out to be forgeries.

Now Hofmann was ready to begin his performance. He had researched what he wanted to write. He had studied and knew hundreds of detailed historical facts about Joseph Smith and his time—tiny things that examiners would look for. Hofmann also knew that he would have to create the document without hesitation. He picked up a steel nib pen and began. His hand produced a free-flowing line. Each letter of each word appeared. Line after line of script was laid down. A brief distraction caused some of the letters to appear shaky. Instead of beginning again, he used a toothpick and volcanic pumice to erase the words and rewrite them. He completed the script. But the document was not finished. Although the paper was genuine, the ink had to look like it was part of the paper. It had to be aged on the paper. Hofmann experimented and discovered that dipping the freshly created document into a chemical bath would turn the ink a rich, aged brown. He used a vacuum to move the ink deep into the paper fibers, which would have happened over time.

Hofmann also knew that letters in the 1830s were not stored flat in filing cabinets. Letters and other documents were usually folded and placed into small, square compartments in desks. So he folded his forgery into thirds.

A good forgery also needed an ownership history, or provenance. He went about creating other fraudulent documents that provided a 150-year chain of ownership from the 1830s to 1981.

Hofmann contacted the Mormon Church and said that he had acquired an important Mormon document called the Joseph III blessing. The church leadership did indeed want this document. They also wanted it examined to see if it was a forgery. Because the Mormon Church had no qualified forensic examiners, they had the Joseph III blessing analyzed by a noted scientist,

Walter McCrone (1916–2002). His findings under the microscope were as follows:

- The paper was made of cotton, hemp, and straw, which suggested that the document was made between 1800 and 1890. (In fact, Hofmann had cut the page from an 1830s volume on Mormon biblical history.)
- The paper also contained mica, an additive that had come into use around 1807.

The microscopist was not a forensic document examiner. He did not evaluate the method and style of the handwriting, nor the ink.

The church tried to confirm Hofmann's claim about where he had acquired the document. Hofmann gave them a signed affidavit—a written statement containing an oath for use as evidence in court. (The affidavit was also a fake.) Church officials checked the name of the person who, in the affidavit, had sold Hofmann the document—Alan Bullock. Hofmann had created this name, but church officials found that an elderly man named Alan Bullock resided in Salt Lake City. Since facts in the affidavit agreed with the address search, church leaders never talked directly to Alan Bullock.

Based upon these preliminary findings, the Mormon Church acquired the Joseph III blessing. A local Mormon businessman, Steven Christensen, was one of Mark Hofmann's clients. Christensen donated the Joseph III blessing to the Mormon Church. Over the years, the church received many donations of sensitive

Mormon documents from Steven Christensen—all through Mark Hofmann.

In 1985, Christensen began to suspect that Hofmann was manufacturing fraudulent documents. Mark Hofmann killed Christensen in a bombing to silence him. During the course of their investigation of Christensen's murder, authorities stumbled onto a mountain of over four hundred suspect or questionable documents—all leading to Mark Hofmann.

The authorities hired two noted forensic examiners, William Flyn and George Throckmorton. They analyzed over 460 Hofmann-connected 1830–1850 documents, including the Joseph III blessing.

In November 1987, Hofmann's trial began in Salt Lake City, Utah. Forensic testimony described that most of the documents shared two unusual marks: microscopic cracking on the surface of the ink, called "alligatoring," and a bright blue glow when placed under ultraviolet light (see Figure 1).

They also noted that inks used to create the questioned documents were iron-gall inks, common from 1800 to 1940. Under ultraviolet (UV) examination, some part of the ink ran from the letters, all in a single direction.

Flyn testified that he tried to duplicate Hofmann's techniques of artificially aging the iron-gall ink applied to genuine paper. He concluded that a chemical had been applied to the inked manuscript, and that the chemical reacted with both the iron pigment and a

FIGURE 1

Cracking Ink and a Blue Glow

(a)

(b)

(a) When Mark Hofmann "aged" his forged documents, he added ammonia. When the ammonia contacted the ink containing gum arabic, it caused the ink to shrink. This produced microscopic cracks as the ink dried. The document examiners called it "alligatoring."

(b) A blue hazing effect was produced when the documents were dipped in the ammonia solution. The hazing effect was visible under ultraviolet light.

common ink additive—gum arabic. Gum arabic is used to make inks thicker. Forensic analysis showed that a chemical base (such as household ammonia) can turn iron inks a very dark brown (simulating age) and cause the gum arabic to go from a liquid to a gel. This gel then formed microscopic cracks as the document dried. Flyn also testified that by observing the document under ultraviolet (UV) light, he could tell that it had been dipped in a chemical solution, then hung up and allowed to dry. This dipping also explained the running ink.

George Throckmorton provided expert testimony regarding other forensic details:

- Some of Hofmann's documents seemed to have been cut with a knife or blade (see Figure 2a).

FIGURE 2

Telltale Marks

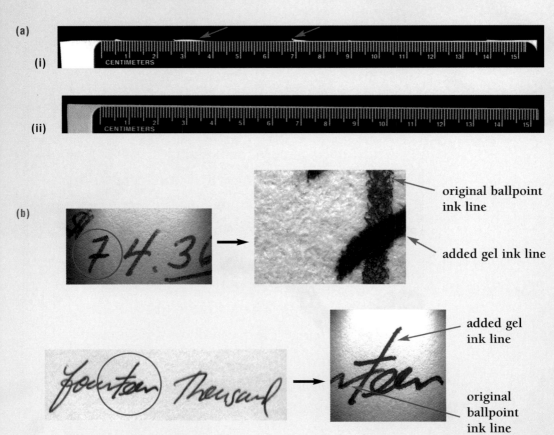

(a) Cut marks can be exposed and viewed by placing the questioned sheet on a flat surface. A ruler is placed over its edge. The edge is examined under a magnifying glass or a microscope. Individual scissor or razor marks can be seen (a-i). Compare these cut edges to the other, uncut edges of the same sheet (a-ii).

(b) Documents can be changed by overwriting words and portions of sentences or by inserting a character, word, or sentence. Here the number $14.36 has been changed to $74.36. The insertion of "teen" changed four thousand to fourteen thousand.

These marks showed that the paper sheet was cut from a book, and was not a single paper stationery sheet—a sign of using a sheet of known age to create a forgery.

- Hofmann dipped his genuine paper in a gelatin solution to "size" it—to prevent the ink from feathering.

The Joseph III blessing, and other Hofmann-sold documents, had many signs of being forged:

- The handwriting had a drawn appearance, with slow, hesitating strokes. Hofmann never resorted to tracing, the dead giveaway to a forgery.
- The other fraudulent documents Hofmann created to prove ownership of the blessing contained over-writing. Overwriting is handwriting that is added afterward to change the meaning of a document (see Figure 2b).

Thanks to the efforts of forensic investigators, Mark Hofmann faced the possibility of a guilty verdict and the death penalty. Instead, he pleaded guilty to lesser charges. He was sentenced to life in prison.

Science and Documents

Forensic science is tested knowledge that can be used in a court of law to discover the truth. A document is a record. It is made up of paper and pigment put together by an instrument such as a pen, pencil, or printer.

A document examiner is a type of forensic scientist. He or she discovers and proves facts about documents. Is a particular document believable? Are its paper and ink of the correct period and kind? Do the facts in the document agree with other known facts? If it is a written or signed document, did the hand of the author create it?

You will use this book as a guide to learning about paper and ink and how they are combined to create a document. You will also learn how to detect whether a document has been forged.

Tools You Will Need

All forensic investigators carry a case notebook. You should too. It will help you collect facts about the cases you are working on and record and organize data.

All of the other materials you will need as a junior forensic investigator can be obtained around the house or in local stores.

Keeping Safe as a Junior Document Investigator

The most important ingredient for success is safety.

1. Be serious about forensic science. An easygoing attitude can be dangerous to you and to others. Always investigate under the supervision of a knowledgeable adult.

2. Read instructions carefully and completely before beginning with any case in this book. Discuss your procedure with a knowledgeable adult before you

start. A flaw in your design could cause an accident. ***If in doubt, check with a science teacher or other knowledgeable adult.***

3. Keep your work area clean and organized. Never eat or drink anything while conducting investigations.
4. Wear protective goggles when working with chemicals or when performing any other experiment that could lead to eye injury.
5. Do not touch chemicals with your bare hands unless instructed to do so. Do not taste chemicals or chemical solutions. Do not inhale vapors or fumes from any chemical or chemical solution.
6. Clean up any chemical spill immediately. If you spill anything on your skin or clothing, rinse it off immediately with plenty of water. Then report what happened to a responsible adult.
7. Keep flammable liquids away from heat sources.
8. Wash your hands after all experiments. Dispose of contaminated waste or articles properly.
9. Be a responsible Web surfer. Explore only genuine topic areas approved by a responsible adult.

All forensic investigators carry a case notebook.
You should too.

How This Book Is Organized

Chapter 1 of this book gave you a true-life example of how one forger, Mark Hofmann, created a document and how forensic document examiners detected his efforts. Chapter 2 gives you important background information about what documents are, the types of materials used to make them, and how they can be altered. You will learn how a forensic document examiner makes an analysis and completes a pretrial report.

In Chapter 3, you will read about true crime cases that involved document scoundrels—deceitful individuals. Learn how forensic science exposed them. Each of these cases has an investigation that will provide you with more forensic skills. It also has recommended science project ideas to practice and expand on what you learn. You may decide to use one of these ideas as a start to your own science fair project.

In Chapter 4, "Investigating the Crime," see if you can create a series of documents that will stump your friends' analyses. You may even want to have them write a pretrial report and present it to other friends acting as a grand jury.

Last, Chapter 5, "Project Analyses," explains the various questions and cases contained in this book.

Let's get to work!

Learning the Secrets of Document Forgery

William Flyn used an important procedure—the scientific method—to discover why the ink on many of Hofmann's suspected documents had cracked. He followed these steps: He made a careful guess (a hypothesis) to explain what he observed. He then designed a method (an experiment) to test his guess, and used his results (data) to conclude whether his guess was correct or whether it should be changed. All forensic scientists use the scientific method to test their ideas and come to a conclusion about a document.

Findings

Forensic scientists must summarize and report their findings (conclusions) to law enforcement authorities and the court. They present formal pretrial reports and verbal testimony.

At times in this book you will be asked to prepare a report to the court. Your pretrial report should contain the following parts and be in this order:

- Observation of data
- Interpretation of data
- Hypothesis

- Testing of hypothesis and procedures followed
- Summary; findings of fact

Your pretrial report should be word-processed, typed, or written clearly in blue or black ink. Most document examiners use photographs to illustrate their findings. They usually present two images—one that has no markings and one that has the points of interest labeled.

Document Analysis

Most of a document examiner's work involves answering questions about a document. Who was the author? Is the document genuine? Was it altered? Have additions been made? Is there evidence of erasures? Sometimes, as in the Hofmann case, a document examiner must use the sciences of optics, physics, and chemistry to find out if inks or paper have been altered.

Document analysis involves many steps:

1. **Researching the document.** A true or genuine document is part of history. A document examiner must research all aspects of the document—its age, the historical relationship of its content with other individuals and documents, authorship, and the materials used to create it.

2. **Learning a document's ownership history.** All documents have an ownership history, beginning with their creation. A document examiner must check the history of a document—finding out who

The Constitution of the United States of America.

Forensic examiners study the paper, ink, and history of a document when determining whether it is genuine.

owned the document during all the years it existed. Many forgers suddenly "come upon" sensational documents. But they have little detailed ownership history to back up their finds. This lack of history about a document is a strong clue that it is a forgery.

3. **Analyzing the paper.** Paper analysis includes determining its age, size, fiber content, and special features such as additives, watermarks, and color.

4. **Analyzing the ink.** Writing inks bind to paper. A document examiner identifies the type of ink used

to make a document. Special analyses can also identify an ink's chemical makeup.

5. **Analyzing the writing tool.** Knowing what type of tool—pen, pencil, or machine—was used to create a document is critical in finding out if the document has been altered or is a fake.

6. **Analyzing the handwriting.** Was the document written by a known writer? A document examiner must be able to see the distinguishing individual writing characteristics that separate one person from everyone else.

7. **Telling the age of a document.** Many times a document examiner is asked to find out the age of a document. The age of a document can sometimes be determined by dating the ink, paper, or watermark. Sometimes a printer's mark or a chance mark can pinpoint a date. Sometimes document examiners use machine-made markings (e.g., dot matrix printers became available in the 1960s) to establish an age limit for a document.

Most of a document examiner's work involves *answering questions* about a document.

Paper Types

Knowledge of papermaking and paper types is essential for a document examiner. You can practice your paper examination skills after reviewing some important facts about paper types.

Popular sheet sizes. The size of a paper sheet tells something about the age of the document. In the eighteenth century, a large full-size sheet of 25 x 38 inches was popular. In the first half of the nineteenth century, the quarto or one-fourth-sheet size (8 x 10 inches) became fashionable. Later, the octavo (4 x 5 inches) was the accepted size for business correspondence. Today, we use the quarto size of 8½ x 11 inches.

Fiber content. All papers are made of close-matted fibers. In the United States, the fiber used to make paper is rag (cotton or linen) and specially treated wood (spruce or pine). Rag fiber is used in the best grades of writing papers. Wood fibers are used in the most inexpensive papers, such as newspaper. Much writing paper uses a combination of these two classes of fibers. Knowing the fiber content allows accurate dating of a sheet of paper. For example, there is no wood pulp in paper of the colonial period. Wood pulp paper was not widely used in the United States until after the American Civil War.

Paper marks: Chain lines and laid lines. In the seventeenth and early eighteenth centuries, paper in the United States was made by hand. When this older

FIGURE 3.

Paper Marks—Chain Lines and Laid Lines

(a)

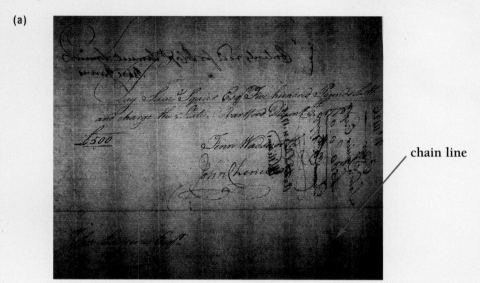

chain line

(b)

laid line

(a) This handmade eighteenth-century paper shows chain lines. Chain lines are marks made in paper by the supporting copper wires of the paper mold. The paper is thinner where these wires contacted the paper, and more transparent (lighter) when held up to the light.

(b) In modern fine writing papers, the closely lined watermark appearance of laid lines are made by parallel wires on a paper-finishing roll.

paper is held up to the light, it shows chain lines. Chain lines are marks made in paper by a mold used to help form each sheet (see Figure 3). Laid lines are closely placed and visible when modern fine writing paper is held up to the light. Laid lines, like chain lines, are marks made by fine wires inserted in the web of a papermaking machine.

Paper marks: Tacking marks. Sometimes forgers treat paper by dipping it in dilute coffee or other fluids. Then they hang individual sheets up to dry using tacks or clothespins, which leave behind marks.

Paper marks: Watermarks. A watermark is used by paper manufacturers to identify their product (see Figure 4). Individual sheets of fine writing paper usually contain watermarks. The watermark is visible when the sheet of paper is held up to a light.

Brightness. Since the 1970s, many papermakers have added optical brighteners to make paper look whiter in room light. They usually print a brightness number (e.g., 84 Bright) on the package. The higher the number, the more brighteners have been added during papermaking.

Paper weight. Papermakers use a weight basis for paper. Paper weight is the weight of 500 sheets, measured in pounds, in that paper's sheet size. Very thin onionskin is 9-pound paper. Quality letter paper (24 pound) is thicker. Most general-use copier paper is 20 pound. Handmade, blotting, and watercolor papers are much thicker and are usually 50 pound.

FIGURE 4.

Watermarks—Old and New

(a)

(b)

(a) A watermark is an image or pattern in paper that appears lighter (more transparent) when held up to light. These watermarks are in handmade paper from the eighteenth century.

(b) Modern watermarks are shown in some paper, including President Abraham Lincoln on the U.S. Series 1999–2003 five-dollar banknote.

●●●●●●●●●●●●●●●●

P R O J E C T :

Practicing Your Paper Analysis Skills

What You Need:

- paper reference collection—at least 4 sheets of each of the following papers: blotting, watercolor, copier, and fine writing
- 4 or more file folders
- fountain pen
- ultraviolet (UV) black light bulb 75W (350–400nm wavelength)
- incandescent bulb
- test paper sheet #1—watercolor paper
- test paper sheet #2—fine writing paper (100% cotton)
- test paper sheet #3—copier paper
- test paper sheet #4—copier paper
- test paper sheet #5—fine writing paper (100% cotton)
- black construction paper
- 10–20X magnifying glass
- clothespin or thumbtack
- scissors
- pencil
- ruler
- coffee
- water
- small tray for diluted coffee
- newspaper
- a friend
- an erasable pen

Before You Begin:

1. Make a paper reference collection. Collect paper reference samples. Your collection should have four sheets each of at least these paper types: blotting, watercolor, copier, and fine writing. Place a sheet of each paper type in a separate file folder. On the folder record the name of the papermaker, sheet size, fiber content, watermark, brightness, weight, and color. Give each folder a number, and number the reference sheet in the folder. Your paper reference collection may contain as many different paper types as you want. Use the collection throughout your investigations in this book.

2. Use scissors to:
   - hand trim test paper sheet #4 (copier paper) to a 4 x 5" octavo size.
   - hand trim test paper sheet #5 (fine writing paper) to an 8 x 10" quarto size.

   Dip the trimmed sample sheet #4 in diluted coffee (1 part coffee in 3 parts water). Ask your friend to dry the small sheet using either a clothespin or thumbtack (and not to tell you which one was used).

3. Assemble one set of five test sheets (#1–#5; see material list). Make pencil marks to identify each sheet so that only you know which ones they are.

4. Use a fountain pen to write the title of this book in the middle of each of the sample sheets.

Identifying the Questioned Samples

Place the five questioned paper samples before a fellow document examiner. Ask your colleague to use a magnifying glass, the analysis steps that follow this list, and your paper reference collection to help in identifying each of the five paper sheets.

- sheet of watercolor paper?
- sheet resembling correspondence paper used in 1824?
- sheet of modern copier paper?
- sheet resembling correspondence paper used in 1889?
- sheet of modern correspondence paper?

1. Use a ruler to measure the paper sheet. Does the sheet size agree with the time period? For example, the folio-sized paper sheet (17 x 24 inches) was the usual size for writing paper in the early eighteenth century. If you were given an 8 x 10-inch document from 1756, you should be suspicious right away.

2. Use a common special effects ultraviolet (UV) black light bulb to view the paper samples in a darkened room. Turn on the black light. Hold the paper up to it. UV light reveals the presence of optical brighteners and other additives mixed into the paper. Paper with optical brighteners and other additives will glow purple under UV light (see Figure 5). (Fluorescent material sensitive to ultraviolet light

FIGURE 5

Modern Papers Have Optical Brighteners

Fine writing paper with optical brighteners will glow purple in UV light.

will absorb its light energy. It then releases this energy in the form of visible light, which makes the object glow purple.) Specialty papers, like watercolor paper, rarely have additives or brighteners added to them.

3. Most writing paper is coated so that inks will not be absorbed by or "bleed" into the fibers. Paper loses its coating over time. Ink applied to older paper will be absorbed into the fibers and show irregular line edges called feathering. Duplicate the feathering effect by writing with a fountain pen on newspaper—uncoated paper. Compare this ink feathering with Figure 6a.

4. You can get a rough idea of a document's age by carefully looking at the paper's color and marks.

Look at the color: Is the paper dull or yellowing? Yellowing is a result of chemicals called lignins (in wood pulp) reacting with light. Also, other environmental factors such as storage and weather conditions can affect how paper changes its color. Sometimes forgers will dip paper into dilute coffee or other fluids to stain it, giving the illusion of aging.

Look for paper marks: Hold each sheet up to the light of an incandescent bulb or a window. Look carefully at the paper. Do you see watermarks (look back at Figure 4)?

5. Analyze a sample of the paper for its fiber content. To do so, carefully tear a small piece off a paper sample. Does it rip cleanly or leave a jagged edge? The harder to tear, the longer the fibers are in the paper. Long fibers create strong paper. Short fibers create smooth texture. Use Figure 7 as a guide in analyzing paper fiber content. Carefully tear a small piece of a paper sample. Place its torn edge against black construction paper (to provide contrast). Use a 10–20X magnifying glass to see individual paper fibers. Longer fibers are cotton (up to 18 mm long). Shorter fibers are wood (up to 3.5 mm long).

Have your friend prepare a written pretrial report to the court. See Chapter 5 for some analysis hints.

FIGURE 6

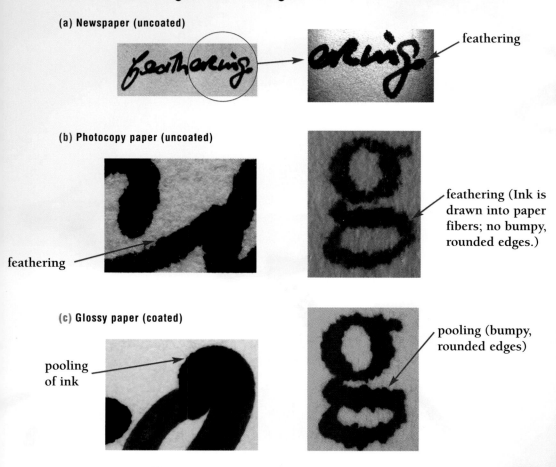

Feathering or Wicking Effect

(a) Newspaper (uncoated)

feathering

(b) Photocopy paper (uncoated)

feathering (Ink is drawn into paper fibers; no bumpy, rounded edges.)

feathering

(c) Glossy paper (coated)

pooling (bumpy, rounded edges)

pooling of ink

(a) Newspaper is uncoated paper. Ink feathering occurs when the ink spreads along the uncoated paper fibers. The ink line will not have a sharp, clean edge.

(b) Uncoated photocopy paper also allows for feathering. The blue ink and the pink ink-jet ink soak into the fibers of the paper.

(c) Glossy, coated paper has special materials on the surface that limit the ink absorbed by the paper fibers. You can see the blue ink has a cleaner edge. However, the coated ink does not allow the ink to soak into the paper; it sits on tops in "pools." These rounded areas of ink that sit on top of the paper dry in rounded patterns. This effect is called wicking.

FIGURE 7

Analyzing Paper Fibers

(a)

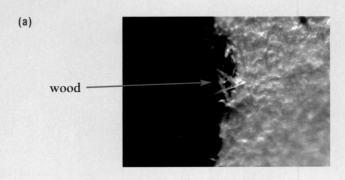

wood

(b)

cotton

(c)

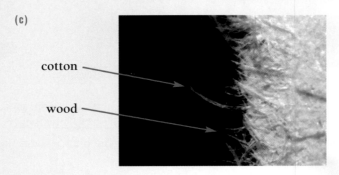

cotton

wood

(a) newspaper (all wood fiber)
(b) writing paper (100 percent cotton fiber)
(c) copier paper (25 percent cotton, 75 percent wood fiber)

Ink Analysis

Inks are fluids or pastes used for printing or writing. Most inks are made of two parts: a colorless liquid called the vehicle, and a colorant. The most popular liquid vehicles are water, alcohol, mineral oil, and vegetable oil. Colorants are made from dyes. Most writing inks dry when the vehicle has evaporated and the paper has absorbed the colorant.

Forgers use hypochlorite—laundry bleach—to remove dye-based inks (e.g., nonpermanent marker); pigment-based inks (e.g., permanent marker) cannot be removed by hypochlorite.

You can measure how fast an ink is absorbed into paper by examining erasable ink. Unlike most writing inks, this ink type is not readily absorbed by paper. Instead, the ink binds only to the surface of the paper. It can then be erased without damaging the paper—but only for a short time. The paper does absorb the ink over time. Experiment to find out just how long the ink absorption process takes.

Document examiners use chemical and image analysis to help them identify the type and makeup of the ink present in a document. Table 1 shows ink lines from various ink types at 60X magnification.

TABLE 1. Guide to Writing Ink Lines

INK TYPE	COMMENTS

CARBON BLACK

Ancient ink. Carbon black is an ink pigment. Today it is used in certain water-based drawing inks (e.g., india ink).

IRON-GALL

Middle Ages. A water-based solution of an iron salt and a tannin (chemical present in bark). Low pH (acid) ink. As ink ages it turns from black to rust color. Ultimately improved 100 years ago to become the modern blue-black ink with the addition of a blue dye.

QUICK-DRYING

1930s. Water-soluble fountain pen inks. Their high pH (11–12) makes them soak quickly into paper, eliminating blotting.

PASTE

1940s. Ballpoint inks are thick and pastelike, made of organic chemical solvents instead of water.

CONTEMPORARY

1970s. Fluid water-based inks used in porous or fiber-tipped pens and rollerball pens.

GEL

1990s. Special water-based inks, many of which are fluorescent.

Writing Tool Analysis

Many kinds of handheld instruments, as well as mechanical and electronic devices, are used to apply ink or pencil (graphite) to paper. With care and practice you can learn to identify each type. Table 2 shows ink lines made from different writing tools at 60X magnification.

Handwriting Analysis

No two people write exactly alike. We all learn a standard method of script (cursive) writing. Over time, we add subconscious changes to our learned writing style so that we can write faster.

If two writings by the same person are compared, there will be similarities without any major dissimilarity. A document examiner must be able to identify individual writing characteristics that separate one person from all others.

To see if two documents were written by the same person, a document examiner needs enough writing samples or "standards" from one person. An examiner can normally compare only capitals with capitals, such as *B*s with *B*s. Capitals cannot be compared with lowercase writing. One capital letter (e.g., *A*) cannot be compared with a different capital letter (e.g., *B*); it can only be compared with itself. The writing samples should be as close to the same age as the questioned document as possible. There should be at least five standards to show the normal range of the individual's handwriting.

TABLE 2. *Guide to Writing Tools*

CATEGORY	TYPE/DATE OF INTRODUCTION	COMMENTS
PEN An instrument that applies liquid ink to a surface	Quill, 6th century A.D.	Quill and nib pens produce a double-track line stroke, having darker margins with uniform distribution of ink.
	Steel nib (dip style), 1830s flowback—	Need to recharge ink supply; quill and steel nib pens thus produce changing ink line widths. Note dark flowback.
	Steel nib (fountain), 1884 flowback—	Ink line width remains constant; no recharging. Note dark flowback.
	Ballpoint, 1945	Even spreading of ink across width of line; usually leaves center indentation markings; sometimes skips. Note ink spot "gooping."
	Rollerball, 1960s	Even spreading of ink across width of line; no indentation marks; line has quality of fountain pen.
	Fiber tip, 1964	Even spreading of ink across width of line; line width varies with size of tip.

continued ⟶

TABLE 2. Guide to Writing Tools *(continued)*

CATEGORY	TYPE/DATE OF INTRODUCTION	COMMENTS
PENCIL An instrument containing a core of solid marking substance within a holder	Graphite, 16th century • hard • medium • soft	Particles of solid graphite cling to paper fibers. The amount of graphite mixed with clay following baking determines hardness.
MECHANICAL A machine that can reproduce printed characters on paper	Typewriter, Adding machines, Calculators, Cash registers; 1870s ⟶ nzan W1 1-9599, (lever strike); 1961 ⟶ r fort (ball strike) ublica	Each manufacturer designed similar typefaces individually. Ink is supplied through a movable ribbon.
ELECTRONIC A computerized output device that records information on paper	Impact printer, 1950s R00208	Type is arranged on a metal type ball or plastic disk (daisy wheel). Ink is supplied through a ribbon.
	Dot matrix, 1960s reet ns Mr. 113	Forms characters as a pattern of dots. Ink is supplied through a ribbon.
	Ink-jet, Laser printer, 1980s st and a st and a st and a	Solid toner electrostatically applied to paper via electronic template. Smudging observed around individual characters.

PROJECT:

Practicing Your Handwriting Analysis Skills

What You Need:

- photocopy machine
- notebook
- pen or pencil
- scissors
- glue stick or white glue
- magnifying glass

Figure 8 shows three writing samples. Can you determine if the questioned writing sample is written by the same person who wrote the known writing samples?

What You Do:

1. Make a photocopy of the compared documents in Figure 8.
2. Copy Table 3 into your notebook. This table will help you organize and compare writing samples from known examples with the unknown (questioned) document.

A document examiner must be able to identify *individual writing* characteristics that separate one person from all others.

FIGURE 8

Known Writing Samples:

SAMPLE 1

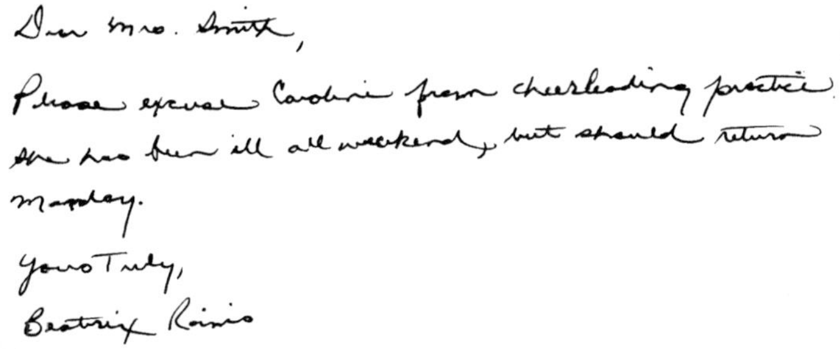

[handwritten]
Dear Mrs. Smith,
Please excuse Caroline from cheerleading practice.
She has been ill all weekend, but should return
Monday.
Yours Truly,
Beatrix Rainis

SAMPLE 2

[handwritten]
Dear Mrs. Smith,
Please excuse Caroline from cheerleading
practice. She has been ill all weekend,
but should return Monday.

Sincerely,
Beatrix Rainis

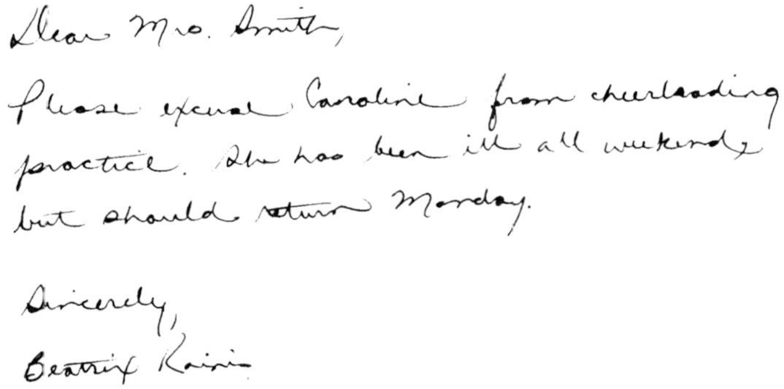

Questioned Writing Sample:

SAMPLE 3

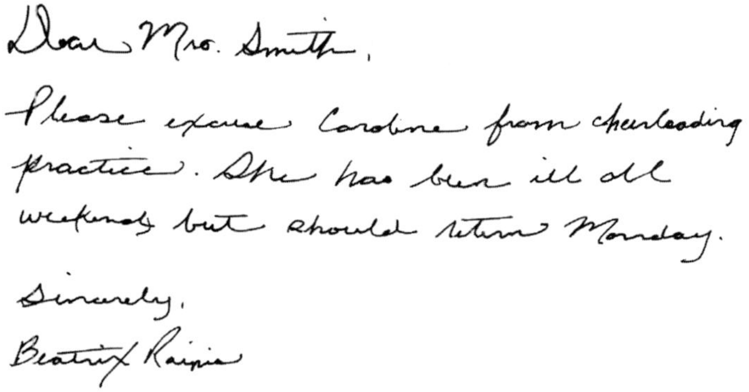

[handwritten]
Dear Mrs. Smith,
Please excuse Caroline from cheerleading
practice. She has been ill all
weekend but should return Monday.
Sincerely,
Beatrix Rainis

Compare the "questioned document" to "known" writing samples.

TABLE 3. Handwriting Comparison Table

WRITING STYLE CHARACTERISTICS	KNOWN WRITING SAMPLE	QUESTIONED WRITING SAMPLE
Word Formation		
Letter Formation		
Quality of line		
Unusual style		

3. Carefully examine each of the known writing examples. Use a magnifying glass if needed to examine fine detail in the cursive writing. Select specific writing examples that illustrate some or all of the points listed for each writing style characteristic (in Step 4).

4. Use the following as a writing style checklist when making your comparison:

Word formation:
- look (form) of an entire word
- slant, from backhand to forehand slope

Letter formation:
- significant matches or mismatches on the form of a particular letter
- fine detail of letter formation
- relative proportions and size of letters

- parts of compound letters, such as *k* and *g*
- links or spaces between each letter

Quality of line:
- quality of the pen line itself. Is it smooth, tremulous, jagged, confident? Does it pause? Are there odd pen lifts?
- relative height of each letter above the line

Unusual style
- parts of letters may be conventional or unusual in style; look for flourishes and ornamentations

5. Use scissors to cut out each selected example and glue it in the appropriate location on your notebook copy of the table, across from its corresponding style characteristic.

6. Repeat Steps 4 and 5 on the questioned document. You may want to use a pencil or pen to mark specific examples with a small arrow.

7. When you are ready to compare your analysis results with the actual results, use the analysis of the handwriting samples in Figure 9 as a guide. Based upon the comparison analysis, the third writing sample was not written by the same person.

    Your analysis (sample comparison table) and conclusions (your expert opinion) should be included in your pretrial report to the court.

FIGURE 9

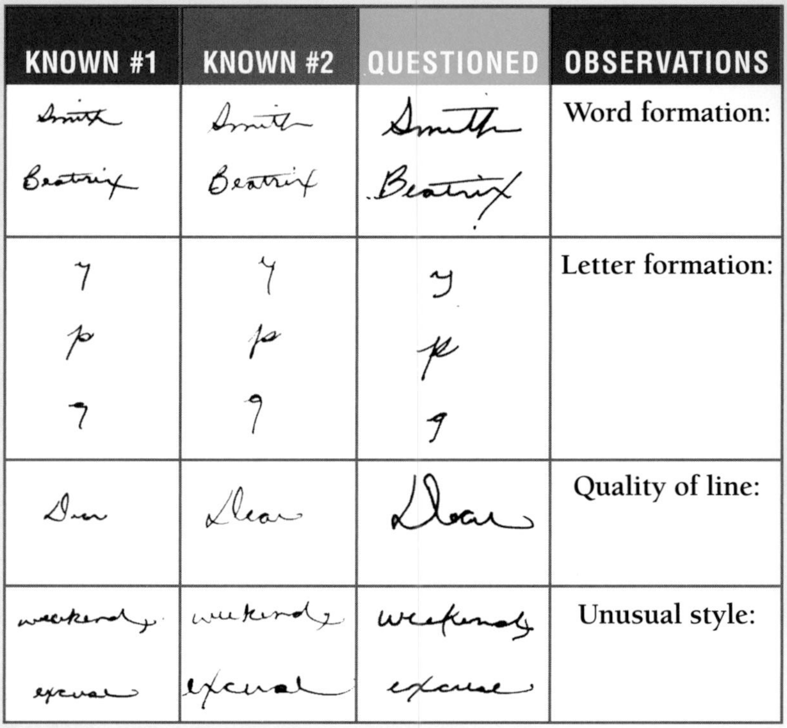

The questioned document is compared to the known writing samples.

KNOWN #1	KNOWN #2	QUESTIONED	OBSERVATIONS
Smith *Beatrix*	*Smith* *Beatrix*	*Smith* *Beatrix*	Word formation:
y *p* *q*	*y* *p* *q*	*y* *p* *q*	Letter formation:
Dear	*Dear*	*Dear*	Quality of line:
weekend *excuse*	*weekend* *excuse*	*weekend* *excuse*	Unusual style:

Exposing an Altered Document

An altered document is one that has been changed in some way. Perhaps someone added a sentence, deleted a number, or substituted one name for another. The document examiner's task is to find that change. Documents can be changed in several ways. The most common ways are removing portions by erasure, covering over using a material such as correction fluid, adding an ink or pencil line(s), or photocopying. Each method requires a separate technique for identification. Table 4 will help you detect these changes.

TABLE 4. Guide to Altered Documents

TECHNIQUE	TYPES	DETECTION
ERASURES	Chemical: Use of a bleaching agent to erase ink	Hold paper in front of UV light in a dark room. UV light reveals staining.
	Abrasive: Use of an eraser or sharp instrument to erase ink	Magnifying glass and oblique (side) lighting reveals disturbance of paper fibers.
OBLITERATION	Use of correction fluid	Hold paper in front of lamp. "Transmitted light" reveals opaque area.
ADDITION	Adding a new stroke or line to an original line in a letter or word; adding additional words	Magnifying glass reveals different line pattern, line break, or jerkiness. • Check for overwriting. (This "1" was changed to a "7".)
		• Check for pen lift— lifting pen or pencil in the middle of a letter or word. pen lift
		hesitation • Check for hesitation strokes.

continued ⟶

TABLE 4. Guide to Altered Documents *(continued)*

TECHNIQUE	TYPES	DETECTION
PHOTOCOPYING	Use of a photocopier to overcopy, enlarge, or reduce in size	Careful examination; expertise of the document examiner based upon the document and interviews • Check for magnification alteration.

• Check for background flaws.

• Check for type incompatibility.

• Check for stray markings. (photocopied ten times)

January 7, 2005

January 7, 2005

44

P R O J E C T :

Practicing Your Altered-Document Detection Skills

What You Need:

- ballpoint pen
- white paper, unlined
- ink eraser
- photocopy machine
- a friend
- correction fluid

What You Do:

1. Use a ballpoint pen to write on a white sheet of unlined paper, "The game is afoot."
2. Use an ink eraser to carefully erase the word *afoot* and write *far afield* in its place.
3. Photocopy the altered document. Can a friend tell if either the original or the photocopy is an altered document?
4. On another sheet of unlined white paper, write "$1,234 dollars and 00/xx cents." Use correction fluid to obliterate the *1* and change it to an *8*. Photocopy this altered document. Can a friend detect that either is an altered document?

Telling the Age of a Document

Most legal documents have a printer's mark—a series of code numbers that gives information about the source and date of the printing (see Figure 10). Such age information can be useful in telling if a document has been altered.

FIGURE 10

●●●●●●●●●●●●●●●●●●●

Printer's Mark

37-3167-05-BU No. 3

Code numbers on printed forms give information about the source and date of printing. In this example, the first group of digits, 37, indicates a 1937 printing of this government form.

●●●●●●●●●●●●●●●●●●

● ● ● ● ● ● ● ● ● ● ● ● ● ●

CHAPTER 3

Inspector's Casebook

The ten cases in this chapter are true crime cases involving document fraud. You will learn how forensic document examiners solved each case. Then you will practice your detection skills to solve a similar case of your own.

CASE # 1

● ● ● ● ● ● ● ● ● ● ● ● ●

The Case of the President's Signature

OBJECTIVE: To practice signature analysis

THE SCOUNDREL: Martin Coneely, alias Joseph Cosey (1887–early 1950s)

THE CRIME: Joseph Cosey was a master forger who spent most of his career in New York. Unlike most other forgers, he never used tracing to create his forgeries. Cosey's specialty was his ability to relax and copy the rhythm and flow of a person's handwriting. He was a careful forger, studying all he could about the facts surrounding the person and the person's connection to the document he was forging. Cosey knew that genuine materials made his forgeries look believable. He cut his own quill pens. He mixed iron fillings with Waterman's® brown ink to simulate iron-gall ink. Genuine paper was also a key feature of Cosey's forged documents.

Cosey forged documents from many individuals—especially Edgar Allan Poe and Abraham Lincoln. In the end it was not paper or his trademark brown ink that did Cosey in—it was a careless Lincoln signature. In January 1934, knowledgeable New York book dealer Edward L. Dean spotted a poor example of Cosey's imitation of Lincoln's handwriting. The forgery did not duplicate a distinctive characteristic of Lincoln's signature (see Figure 11).

As you can see, Lincoln crafted his signature in three levels: the capital *A*, the *Linco*, and the *ln*. Cosey's Lincoln signature is on one level.

When arrested on January 11, 1934, Cosey had a bottle of brown ink and forged manuscripts by Poe and Lincoln. Cosey pleaded guilty and was sent to prison for three years.

Document experts estimate that many of Cosey's forgeries are still undetected—quietly resting in the vaults of many libraries and educational institutions.

PROJECT:
A Closer Look at Signatures

What You Need:
- sheets of white paper
- tracing paper

FIGURE 11

Joseph Cosey and Abraham Lincoln Signatures

(a)

(b) (i)   (ii)

(a) This genuine Abraham Lincoln signature shows his unique three-level signature. Level 1 contains the down strokes of the *A*. Notice that the base of the *A* is slightly lower than the rest of the signature. Level 2 includes the writing of the *Linco*. Level 3, the highest level of the signature, contains the letters *ln*.

(b) Joseph Cosey made the mistake of writing Lincoln's forgery all on one level.

(i)   Joseph Cosey forgery

(ii) Abraham Lincoln signature (genuine)

- **ballpoint pen**
- **signatures of the known and unknown (Figure 12)**
- **friends**

A person's signature is a very personal matter—it is his or her individual legal mark.

What You Do:

1. On a clean sheet of white paper, use a pen to write your signature in a natural way. On another clean sheet of paper, write your name with your eyes closed. Compare both signature groups. Although no two signatures are ever identical, can you see that both closely resemble each other?

2. In your notebook, list four or five script characteristics of your signature (e.g., like those of Lincoln's). On another clean sheet of paper, write your signature, with your eyes open, at least ten times. Does each signature have those unique script characteristics?

3. Place a piece of tracing paper over the sheet containing your first, eyes-open signature. Use a pen to trace it. Now compare this tracing to the original. Is the copied signature line hesitant and jerky, even though you made it yourself?

4. Have your friends practice your signature. Can they create a convincing forgery?

5. See if you can detect genuine signatures of two individuals in Figure 12, which includes one from President Martin Van Buren. Chapter 5 has the analysis findings.

Science Project Idea

Collect five examples of a friend's signature. Mark these as known. Have your friend give you an autograph on a clean sheet of paper made with his or her eyes closed. On five other clean sheets of paper, ask your friend to try to write disguised signature examples. Use a magnifying glass to examine each of the signatures. See if you can find similarities between the known, closed-eye, and disguised samples—proving that all the signatures were made by the same hand. You might want to make enlarged photocopies for an illustrated pretrial report.

FIGURE 12

Signatures of the Known and Unknown

(a) Known

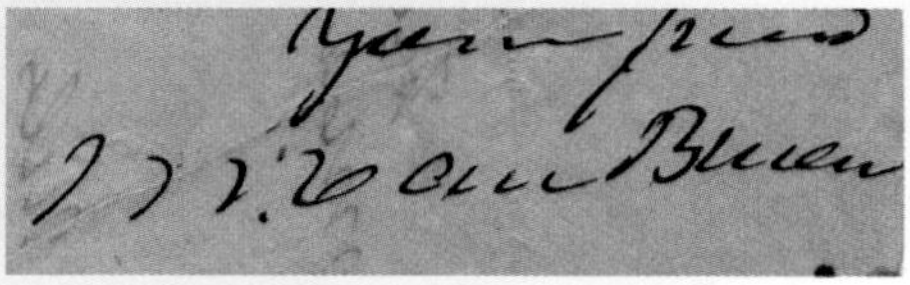

(b) Unknown

1.

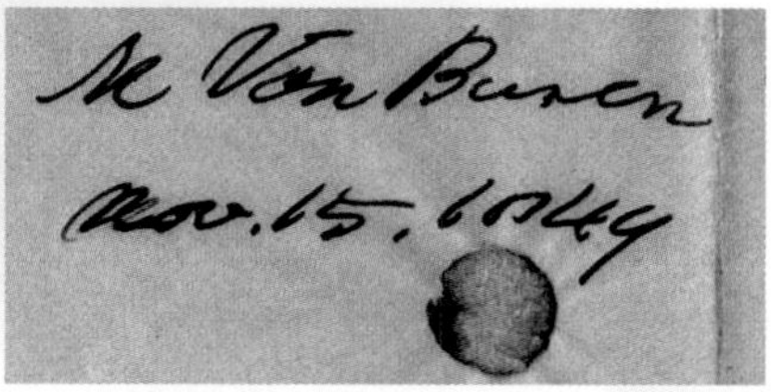

2.

3.

4.

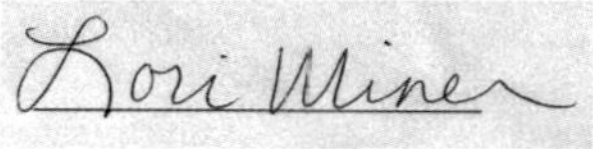

(a) These are two genuine signatures, one of President Martin Van Buren and one of a woman named Lori Miner. Use these authentic examples as a guide in analyzing the unknown signatures in (b).

(b) Can you pick out the genuine signatures?

The Case of the Deadly Message Label

OBJECTIVE: To learn more about inks using a technique called chromatography

THE SCOUNDREL: John Magnuson (1878–?)

THE CRIME: On December 27, 1922, Marshfield, Wisconsin, resident James Chapman received a package in the mail. He thought it was a late Christmas gift. When he opened it, the package exploded, killing his wife, Clementine. James Chapman lost a hand. Police recovered a portion of the address label.

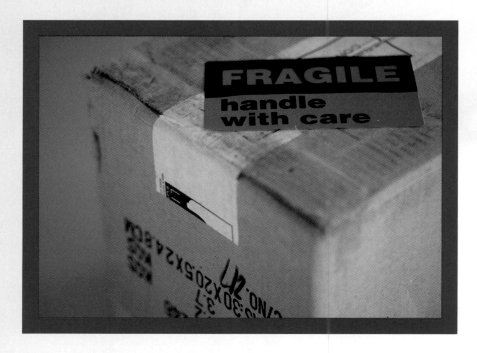

The pieces of the address label were painstakingly put back together. It said: "J.A. Chapman, R.1, Marsfilld, Wis." A handwriting expert who examined the label, John Tyrell, thought that the misspelling of *Marshfield* was a valid mistake—not disguised writing. His opinion was that an immigrant, probably from Sweden, wrote the label. (The Swedish language does not use the sounds *sh* and *ie*.) The only Swedish immigrant living in the community was John Magnuson.

Tyrell did a special analysis of the ink on the label. He identified it as Carter's black ink. He also noted that a medium smooth-pointed fountain pen nib was used.

Tyrell's expert opinion was enough to convince a judge to issue a search warrant. In a search of Magnuson's home, police found a fountain pen with a medium smooth-pointed nib and filled with Carter's black ink. A Milwaukee forensic chemist analyzed the ink from the recovered label. He found it to be a unique mix of colorants that matched the ink found in John Magnuson's pen. Magnuson, the "Yule Bomb Killer," was sentenced to life imprisonment on March 31, 1923.

PROJECT:
Analyzing Writing Inks

What You Need:
- **4 pens with different water-soluble black and blue inks (e.g., fountain pen, Flair®, Pilot®, and Uni-Ball® brands)**
- **white coffee filter (large size)**

- **tape or paper clip**
- **pencil**
- **2 plastic cups**
- **scissors**
- **water**
- **a friend**

Since the late 1950s, a laboratory technique called chromatography, or "color writing," has been used to identify dye components. You can make chromatographs of different pen inks. By analyzing these chromatographs, you will be able to tell what colorants are in different ink samples.

What You Do:

Use Figure 13 as a guide when making an ink chromatogram.

1. Cut out four strips of filter paper, each 6 x 3/4 inches (15 x 2 cm). Cut a point on one end of each strip.
2. Place a small spot of black ink from a black ink fountain pen near the pointed end of one of the filter papers and allow it to dry. Repeat this step on the different paper strips with the three remaining ink sources (e.g., Flair®, Uni-Ball®, and Pilot® brands). Use a pencil to write the name of the pen type on the top of each filter paper strip.
3. Fill a plastic cup with about 1 inch (2 to 3 cm) of water. Attach one paper strip to a pencil using tape or a paper clip (see Figure 13a). Position the paper strip so that it hangs in the center of the cup without touching the sides. Place only the *tip* of the spotted

FIGURE 13

Making a Chromatogram of Black Ink from a Flair Porous-Tip Pen

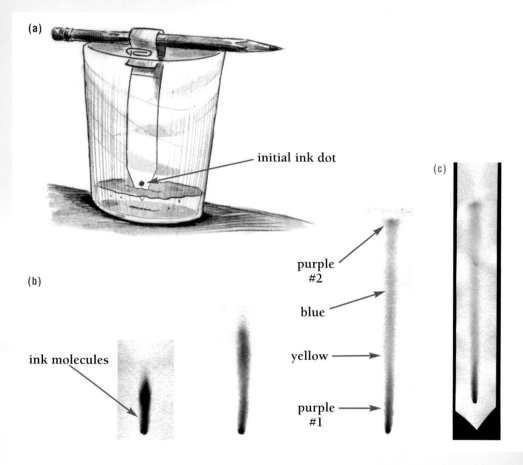

(a)

initial ink dot

(c)

(b)

purple
#2

blue

ink molecules

yellow

purple
#1

(a) Place a small spot of ink sample near the bottom of the strip. Hang the paper strip so that its point just touches the water. Do not let the ink spot go under the water.

(b) Watch the water rise and carry the ink molecules. You can see that this "black" ink is really made of four colors: purple #1, yellow, blue, and purple #2.

(c) Your finished chromatogram may look like this one.

end of the filter paper into the water. Do not let the ink spot touch the water. The water will rise up the filter paper. When it reaches the ink spot, it will continue rising with or without some of the ink.

Do the dye colors that make up the ink separate as the water moves up the filter paper? The lighter (smaller) dye molecules travel farthest on the filter paper; heavier (larger) dye molecules do not travel as far. The resulting image is called a chromatogram. A chromatogram is like a fingerprint, a visual way to show all the individual dye colorants present in an ink sample, separated by their molecular size.

4. Repeat Step 3 with each of the other three ink samples to create a beginning reference collection of water-soluble inks.

5. Ask a friend to compare these four "known" chromatograms to the "unknown" chromatograms in Figure 14. Can you identify any of the unknowns? See Chapter 5 for analysis findings.

Science Project Idea

Make chromatograms of the water-based colored inks from various manufacturers. Through chromatographic analysis, find out how many different ink colorants are in each ink color. If possible, have an adult help you scan these dried chromatograms into a computer (make a digital image) to create an ink database of manufacturer's ink colorants. Do different manufacturers use the same ink colorants?

FIGURE 14

Water-Soluble Ink Chromatograms by Brand

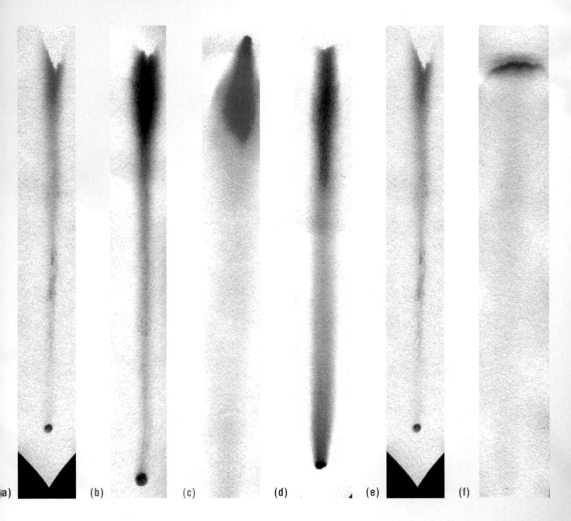

(a) (b) (c) (d) (e) (f)

Can you use your chromatograms, along with the one in Figure 13c, to help you identify the unknown, water-soluble inks in this figure? (See page 107 for results.)

●●●●●●●●●●●●●●●●

The Case of the Implicating Impression

OBJECTIVE: To investigate paper indentations

THE SCOUNDREL: William Henry Podmore (1900–1930)

THE CRIME: William Henry Podmore worked for fifty-seven-year-old Vivian Messiter, an oil company agent in Southampton, England. He regularly wrote receipts to customers. He also regularly stole money from the company.

In the spring of 1929, Podmore feared that Messiter would discover his ongoing withdrawals of company money. He murdered his employer to silence him. Months later, Messiter's decaying body was found in a garage behind some boxes. The medical examiner determined that he had died from blows to the head. A hammer was the murder weapon.

To remove any trace that placed him at the scene of the crime, Podmore tore off pages from the company receipt book. He had written on these pages the day he murdered Messiter. A dated receipt, written in Podmore's handwriting, would have proved he had been at the murder scene. Podmore thought that by removing all the receipt copies written by him, he would be removing any evidence of his presence at work on the day of the murder.

Podmore did not realize he was still leaving behind evidence. The top sheet of the *next* unwritten receipt contained the indented impression of his handwriting, including the date.

The police investigated the murder. The sales receipt book was found. They viewed the company receipt book using side lighting. It revealed the physical link of Podmore to the crime scene. Photographs of Podmore's writing were presented in court. Convicted, he was sent to Winchester prison. He was hanged on April 22, 1930.

PROJECT:
Revealing Indented Writing

What You Need:
- ballpoint pen or pencil
- soft lead pencil with a sharp point
- pad of paper
- desk lamp
- a friend

What You Do:

1. Have a friend use either a ballpoint pen or a sharp pencil to write or print a lengthy note on the top sheet of a pad of paper. Make sure that your friend writes normally and does not press down too hard on the paper. Have your friend then remove the top sheet on the pad. It will be used to confirm your analysis.

2. Using a soft (No. 1 or 2) pencil, rub graphite over the left half of the next (clean) sheet of paper on the pad. Can you detect any indented writing?

3. Hold the pad of paper horizontally about eight inches under a desk lamp. Slowly tip the pad toward you to obtain side lighting. Can you read the rest of the message using side lighting (light shining on the object from the side, revealing marks and indentations in the paper)? In your notebook, write the message if you see it.

4. Repeat Steps 2 and 3 with the next (clean) sheet of paper from the pad. Can you use the graphite or side lighting technique to detect indented writing?

Which technique is more effective—graphite rubbing or side lighting—in revealing indented writing? See Chapter 5 for analysis findings.

CASE # 4

The Case of the Signature That Was Not Real

OBJECTIVE: To detect stamped signatures

THE SCOUNDREL: Carl Nanni

THE CRIME: Carl Nanni was an accountant living in Rochester, New York. One of his many clients was AJS Merchandising. As one of his accounting responsibilities, Nanni wrote company checks and prepared tax returns for John Sureaz, AJS's owner.

In 1987, the Internal Revenue Service (IRS) began an investigation of the company's tax filings. The investigator, Barbara Ricotta, could not locate Sureaz. The 1983 and 1984 tax returns had Sureaz's stamped signature, but no Social Security number. The 1986 company tax return bore a written Sureaz signature.

Ricotta had also reviewed Nanni's personal tax returns and was familiar with his signature. Ricotta had asked Nanni why none of the AJS returns had Sureaz's Social Security number. Nanni said that he had told Sureaz to write it on the returns.

Ricotta thought that the Sureaz signature and Nanni's had many similarities. Things just did not add up. Ricotta concluded that there was a possible conspiracy to take money from the corporation. She recommended that the IRS begin a fraud investigation.

By July 1990, the government had found that the name "John Sureaz" did not exist in IRS, Social Security, or state department of motor vehicle files.

During his trial in 1993, Carl Nanni said he wrote most of the checks for AJS Merchandising and that he used a stamp for the signature of John Sureaz. He told the court that he only used the stamp when Sureaz told him to.

Nanni gave differing testimony about Sureaz. One time he described Sureaz as weighing between 160 and 175 pounds. Another time he said he was between 135 and 140 pounds. When asked how he got the signature

stamp, Nanni first said that Sureaz had brought the stamp, and that Nanni's office had neither requested nor ordered it. Later, he testified that he had ordered the stamp.

The court required Carl Nanni to provide some writing samples for evaluation by a document examiner. The expert identified Nanni as the original writer of the stamped Sureaz signatures, and of Sureaz's hand-written signature, confirming Ricotta's suspicions. Carl Nanni was given a thirty-two-month sentence for filing false income tax returns for AJS Merchandising, Inc.

PROJECT:
Detecting Stamped Signatures

What You Need:
- photocopier
- scissors
- glue stick or white glue
- magnifying glass
- transparent acetate sheets

Stamped signatures are legal signatures—if they are used under the direction of the signature holder. Stamped signatures are common on certificates, banknotes, checks, and other documents.

A stamped signature can be made by engraving a signature line into a wood or metal plate, or by creating a rubber stamp—like an address stamp. King Henry VIII (1491–1547) allowed the use of a wooden stamp for some of his documents. He appointed three men of his council to be allowed to "stamp for the King."

Examining stamped signatures at 10X magnification shows certain common features:

- lines of a stamped signature are usually thick and do not change in width; see Figure 15a.
- a stamped signature has small breaks in the ink; see Figure 15b.
- a stamped signature does not have darkened areas where a line crossover occurs (e.g., when crossing a *t* in ink, the area where the two lines meet is darker); see Figure 15c.

As a forensic document examiner, you are being consulted by an autograph dealer to find out if the signatures in Figure 16 are genuine or stamped.

What You Do:

1. Copy Table 5 into your notebook.
2. Use a photocopier to make four standard copies of Figure 16.

FIGURE 15

A Closer Look at Stamped Signatures

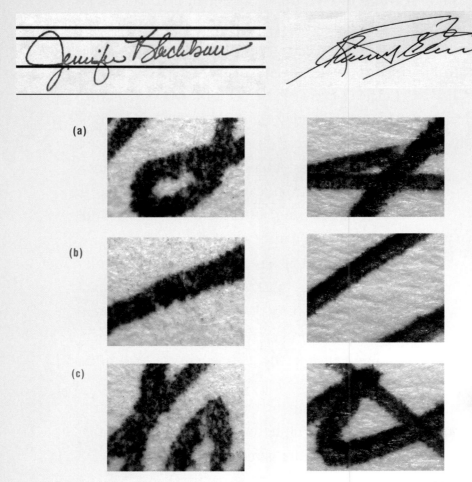

Compare a magnified view of a portion of a stamped signature (left) to a similar magnified view of an ink hand signature (right).

(a) Ink line. It is uniform in a stamped signature; it varies in a hand signature.

(b) Line breaks. There are breaks in a stamped signature; no breaks in a hand signature.

(c) Crossover marks. There are no marks in a stamped signature; there are darker crossover marks in a hand signature.

3. Using a magnifying glass and the signature analysis table, determine which signatures in Figure 16 are stamped and which are genuine.

4. Cut and paste copies of signatures that illustrate each line characteristic. Use the table as a visual guide to writing your report. See Chapter 5 for analysis findings.

TABLE 5. Signature Analysis Table

CHARACTERISTIC	OBSERVATION
• Ink line varies	Signature a Signature b Signature c
• Line uniformly bold	Signature a Signature b Signature c
• Examination shows small breaks in the ink	Signature a Signature b Signature c
• Examination shows crossover marks	Signature a Signature b Signature c

FIGURE 16

Are these signatures handwritten or stamped?

(a)

(b)

(c)

SNED BY

Many individuals who write a lot of letters or who are sought after for their signature often sign their name using a mechanical device called an autopen. Autopen patterns are easy to spot. An autopen holds a ballpoint pen at a 90-degree angle, making every stroke the same width. Examine the two signatures of Bill Clinton in Figure 17. Photocopy these two signatures onto transparent acetate sheets. Place one acetate sheet over the other and inspect for an identical match. If you find an identical match, it is an autopen pattern. Autograph dealers routinely do this to detect autopen signatures in collections they acquire. Are these signatures genuine?

FIGURE 17

Bill Clinton Autopen Signatures?

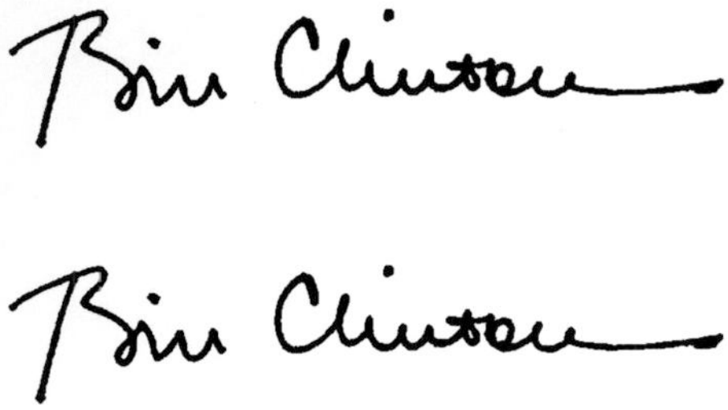

Are these genuine or autopen signatures?

The Case of the Windsor Note

OBJECTIVE: To use ultraviolet light for document examination

THE SCOUNDRELS: Wesley Weber, Anthony Caporale, Dustin Kossom, and Ryan Hodare

THE CRIME: Beginning in the spring of 2000, and into 2001, storeowners in Ontario and Quebec, Canada, began seeing many high-quality counterfeit $100 banknotes. The forgeries were so prevalent that many businesspeople stopped accepting $100 and $50 Canada banknotes.

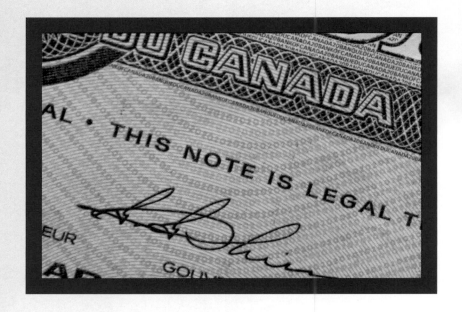

Since that spring in 2000, the RCMP Bureau for Counterfeit and Document Examination in Ottawa examined over 38,000 suspect Bank of Canada notes. These notes had all been given to unsuspecting small businesspeople.

The bureau found:

- All the notes were printed on the same ink-jet printer with the same printing defects.
- The paper was 100 percent cotton, cream-colored, and not watermarked.
- The paper was treated so that it would not glow purple under UV light. It appeared that some kind of clear coating had been applied to the paper.
- A fluorescent ink was applied to imitate the small green dots applied randomly on genuine bills. Although the ink glowed under UV light, it could be scratched off the counterfeit notes.

The bureau determined that the printing characteristics of these counterfeit $100 notes were similar to a counterfeit $20 note made in Windsor, Ontario. In Windsor, the police had a suspect—Wesley Weber. They decided to monitor him closely.

On July 12, 2001, the authorities searched a rented lakeside home in Belle River, just outside Windsor. Computers, paints, UV inks, paper, and an ink-jet printer were seized. Over 2,000 Bank of Canada $100 notes were also seized. Weber and his accomplices were convicted of counterfeiting. He was sentenced to five years in prison; his accomplices, two.

PROJECT:
Using Ultraviolet Light to Examine Documents

What You Need:

- 4 paper types (available at an office supply store):
  - paper sample #1—white laser or copier paper with 80+ brightness value
  - paper sample #2—white laser or copier paper with lower than 80 brightness value
  - paper sample #3—white 100 percent cotton business paper (Southworth® brand)
  - paper sample #4—white 25 percent cotton business paper (Southworth® brand)
- can of clear acrylic spray (Krylon® brand)
- 4 ink types (available at an office supply store):
  - ink sample #1—gel ink, fluorescent orange (Papermate® brand)
  - ink sample #2—blue fountain pen ink
  - ink sample #3—yellow Hi-Liter® pen
  - ink sample #4—pink Hi-Liter® pen
- UV black light bulb—75W (350–400 nm wavelength)
- shallow pan
- bottled water
- scissors
- clothespins
- clothesline (outdoor)
- pencil
- an adult

What You Do:

1. Copy Table 6 into your notebook. In your table you will record your experiment results.

2. Using scissors, cut one sheet of each of four paper samples into two equal pieces. Use a pencil to label a corner of each sheet with the sample number (e.g., *1a* or *1b*) and paper type (e.g., copier paper 80+ brightness).

3. Using clothespins, hang the four *b* samples on an outdoor clothesline. **Have an adult** spray the center of each sheet, on both sides, with Krylon® clear acrylic. Let the paper dry for 20 minutes. These are the treated paper samples. The purpose of the acrylic spray is to see whether the sprayed area will not glow purple under UV light.

4. In a darkened room, turn on the black light (UV light source). Hold each of the eight numbered paper samples under the UV light. Record the effect of the acrylic spray. Does the area of the paper that was sprayed with acrylic look different? Did the acrylic spray affect the optical brighteners?

5. Write a pretrial report that discusses the following:
   - Do all examined copier papers contain optical brighteners?
   - Do all examined fine writing papers have optical brighteners?

TABLE 6. Data for UV & White Light Examination of Documents

	COLOR (room light)	COLOR (UV light)
Paper sample 1a Description		
Paper sample 1b Description		
Paper sample 2a Description		
Paper sample 2b Description		
Paper sample 3a Description		
Paper sample 3b Description		
Paper sample 4a Description		
Paper sample 4b Description		
Ink sample 1a		
Ink sample 1b		
Ink sample 2a		
Ink sample 2b		
Ink sample 3a		
Ink sample 3b		
Ink sample 4a		
Ink sample 4b		

- Under UV light, can you tell the difference between a paper with low and high brightness values?
- How effective is coating a sheet with clear acrylic in removing (or dulling) the purple UV glow made by optical brighteners?

6. Using scissors, cut another sheet of white 100 percent cotton business paper into two equal pieces. Use a pencil to label them *a* and *b*.

7. On each sample (*a* and *b*), use four types of ink to write out the description of each ink. Use Figure 18 as a guide:

  - Ink sample #1—fluorescent orange gel ink
  - Ink sample #2—blue fountain pen ink
  - Ink sample #3—yellow Hi-Liter® ink
  - Ink sample #4—pink Hi-Liter® ink

FIGURE 18

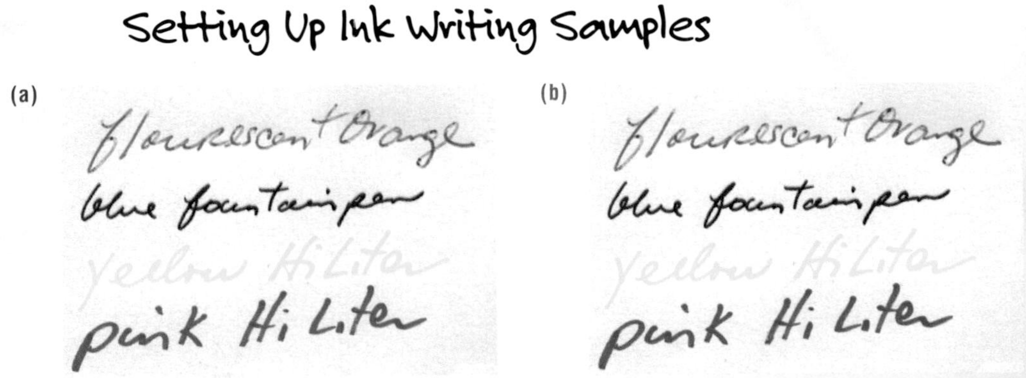

Setting Up Ink Writing Samples

(a)

(b)

floureScent Orange
blue fountain pen
yellow HiLiter
pink Hi Liter

floureScent Orange
blue fountain pen
yellow HiLiter
pink Hi Liter

Paper samples (a) and (b) each have four ink samples on them: fluorescent orange gel ink, blue fountain pen ink, yellow Hi-Liter® ink, and pink Hi-Liter® ink.

73

8. Place the *b* sample in a pan of bottled water overnight. Use a clothespin to hang it up to dry.

9. After drying, examine both paper samples under white (room) light, and then under UV light. Write your observations in your notebook data table.

10. Write a pretrial report that discusses the following:
    - Does placing a document in water for long periods remove some inks?
    - What do you learn about an ink that can and an ink that cannot be removed by water?
    - Can an ink line invisible in room light be made visible?
    - Do all inks contain a fluorescent colorant?
    - What kind of result would you get if you made a chromatogram (see Case #2) of each of the sample inks?

    See Chapter 5 for charts and analysis.

Science Project Ideas

- If possible, use a UV light source to examine a personal check and U.S. or Canadian banknotes (series 1999 and 2004 U.S. $20 banknotes, or 1986 Canadian $2 banknote). How many examples of UV active and dull areas can you observe?

- Add to your reference collection (Chapter 2) by selecting samples of various copier and ink-jet printer paper. Are all of these papers "modern"—do they have added optical brighteners?

The Case of the Questioned Photocopy

OBJECTIVE: To practice analysis of photocopied documents

DOCUMENT EXAMINER: Ordway Hilton (1913–1998)

BACKGROUND INFORMATION: A photocopy is a reproduction of an original document. When a forged document is photocopied, small defects such as erasures and paste lines can be eliminated. With any questioned document, examining the original document is always best. If that cannot happen, examination of a direct copy (a first-generation photocopy) of the original document will be the most accurate.

When any photocopy is made, small changes in letter size and spacing will occur. If a photocopy of another photocopy is made, these differences become even more noticeable.

In some cases, copying two documents (one on top of the other) to produce a new "original" copy (called overcopying) can produce stray marks or change the size of letters and letter spacing. These marks are signs of document tampering. Figure 19 shows how fraudulent photocopies can be identified.

FIGURE 19

Analyzing Photocopied Documents

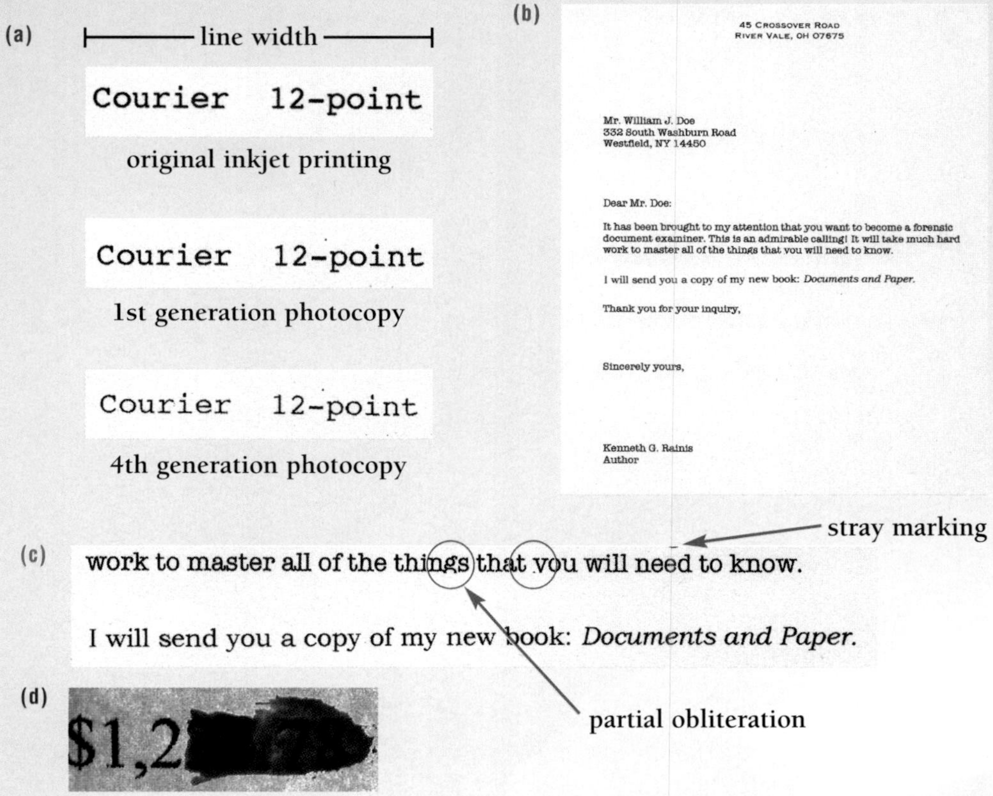

(a)

|————— line width —————|

Courier   12-point

original inkjet printing

Courier   12-point

1st generation photocopy

Courier   12-point

4th generation photocopy

(b)

45 CROSSOVER ROAD
RIVER VALE, OH 07675

Mr. William J. Doe
332 South Washburn Road
Westfield, NY 14450

Dear Mr. Doe:

It has been brought to my attention that you want to become a forensic document examiner. This is an admirable calling! It will take much hard work to master all of the things that you will need to know.

I will send you a copy of my new book: *Documents and Paper.*

Thank you for your inquiry,

Sincerely yours,

Kenneth G. Rainis
Author

(c)

stray marking

work to master all of the things that you will need to know.

I will send you a copy of my new book: *Documents and Paper.*

(d)

partial obliteration

$1,2

(a) Photocopying a document alters both character size and spacing. You can use a transparent metric scale ruler to measure the line width, capital letter "C" height, lowercase letter "i" height, and the spacing between "1" and "2" in each generation photocopy.

(b) This document is not an original; it is an altered photocopy. It has been altered by inserting a line "I will send you a copy of my new book: *Documents and Paper.*" Note that the lower portions of the "g" and the "y" are cut off by a piece of paper containing the overcopied sentence.

(c) Stray marking and partial obliterations indicate that this document is not an original.

(d) This example shows obliteration with the application of correction fluid, when the paper is held up to light.

PROJECT:
Analyzing a Photocopied Document

What You Need:

- computer with a word processing program
- fine writing paper (Southworth® brand, available at office supply store)
- glue stick
- correction fluid
- access to a photocopier
- porous-tip pen, black ink
- magnifying glass
- clear ruler
- a friend
- an adult
- fountain pen
- scissors

What You Do:

You will be simulating an actual crime that occurred in 1969, taken from the case files of Ordway Hilton, a document examiner. You will create two documents, then combine and overcopy the two to create a forgery. See if your handiwork is good enough to stump your friend's analysis.

1. Have an adult help you create part of a business letter on fine writing paper. You will use a computer word processing program. Business letters in the 1960s were usually made using a typewriter. Create your document using 12-point Courier typeface—popular on many typewriters. The letter should

have a heading, inside address, salutation, and a two-paragraph body. Leave off the complimentary close, name, and title. Use the date November 6, 1969. Address it to Señor J.C. Lesley, Guatemala, Guatemala, C.A.

2. With permission, replace the standard copier paper in a computer printer with several sheets of fine writing paper. Print out the letter.

3. Use the computer to create another letter document. Here, you will only be typing the name and person's title. Use 12-point Courier typeface. For the name, type in "M. D. Cure," and for the title, "Vice Presidente Ejecutivo."

4. Use a fountain pen to sign "M. D. Cure" over the typed name. Use scissors to cut the signature line, name, and title from the sheet of paper in a rectangle of 1 x 2 inches.

5. Use a glue stick to affix the signature line, name, and title to the letter created in Step 1. Use correction fluid to eliminate any paste lines or other stray markings.

6. Make a photocopy of the combined document.

7. Give this photocopy to a friend. Can your friend determine if it is genuine or a fraud? Suggest that your friend use a ruler, magnifying glass, and Figure 19 as a guide. See Chapter 5 for analysis results.

Science Project Idea

Create a word-processed original document. Make repeated copies (a copy of a copy) of the printed original document—at least ten times. Use a pencil to number each of these photocopies, beginning with the first photocopy (#1).

Examine each of the copies with a magnifying glass or a computer microscope. Write a pretrial report that analyzes how particular letters, and the spaces between letters, change over this copying process. Is the tenth copy as crisp as the first copy of the original document? Why should only original documents be forensically examined?

The Case of the Paper Crease

OBJECTIVE: To detect the sequence of writing on a document

THE SCOUNDREL: George Barrell

THE CRIME: George Barrell of Willing, Delaware, borrowed money from Mrs. Weaver to buy a house. This type of loan is called a mortgage. In the mortgage document, Mr. Barrell promises to make regular payments to Mrs. Weaver until the loan is paid off.

On January 3, 1923, Barrell altered a mortgage payment receipt. He wrote "in full balance of Mortgage" above the signature of the mortgage holder, Mrs. Weaver. By inserting this statement above her signature, George Barrell could claim that he had paid the full balance of his home mortgage, and that he did not owe Mrs. Weaver any more money. Mrs. Weaver stated that this written statement was not there when she signed the receipt.

The questioned document was presented to a forensic document examiner, who determined that the contested line of script was written after the document had been folded. The act of folding the paper disrupted the mat of paper fibers. When ink was applied to this folded area, it spread out or ran into the fold (see Figure 20). The running of the fluid ink into the fold shows that the line was added *after* the folding of the receipt. If the fold in the paper had been made before the addition of the payment statement, Mrs. Weaver's signature would have shown a similar running or feathering along the fold. Mr. Barrell was charged with fraud and sent to prison.

FIGURE 20

Writing Sample: Case of the Paper Crease

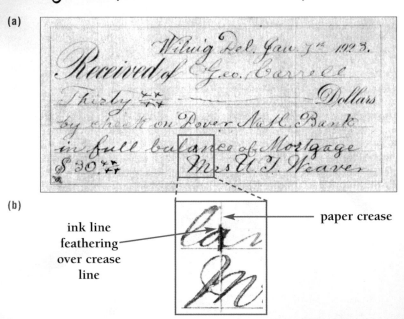

(a)

(b)

ink line feathering over crease line

paper crease

(a) The line entry reading "in full balance of Mortgage" was being disputed by Mrs. Weaver. She said that these words were not there when she signed the receipt.

(b) This magnified view (60X) of the fold area shows the ink feathering of the letter *a* in balance into and along the fold. Note that the *M* in Mrs. has no feathering. The receipt was signed before it was folded. The added line "in full balance of Mortgage" was added after it was folded.

PROJECT:

The Case of the Peculiar Letter "t"

What You Need:

- 2 sheets of white copier paper
- fountain pen with blue ink
- pencil
- magnifying glass
- a friend

All of us have individuality in our handwriting. Abraham Lincoln, as did others in the nineteenth century, crossed his lowercase *ts* from right to left. This is not a common writing practice today. Lincoln regularly used a steel nib dip-style pen. Steel nibbed pens, including today's fountain pens, produce a line characteristic called flowback (see Table 2). It is a darkened ink area at the end of a written line as the nib is removed from the paper. When present, it shows which part of a line was written last.

See if your friends can detect the writing direction in crossing cursive lowercase *ts*.

What You Do:

1. Use a pencil to label a sheet of white copier paper Sheet #1. In cursive, write the following text using a fountain pen and blue ink.

The network of patterns of known writings in these two sets of documents is totally tantalizing.

2. Use a magnifying glass to review each lowercase *t* in the written line. Were all the crossed lines of the lowercase *ts* drawn from left to right? Can you observe flowback on these lines?

3. Use a pencil to label a second white sheet of copier paper Sheet #2. In cursive, write the same sentence as in Step 1, but take care to cross lowercase *ts* from right to left.

4. Use the magnifying glass to examine the lines of the lowercase *ts*. Can you see flowback on the left end of the line?

5. Show these two sheets to your friends. Ask them to examine the two lines of writing with a magnifying glass. See if they notice anything peculiar about the lowercase *ts*.

• •

The Case of the Misdirected Tax Payment

OBJECTIVE: To detect evidence of document alterations

THE SCOUNDREL: Peter Odafe Obebeduo (1958–   )

THE CRIME: In 1991, thirty-three-year-old Bronx, New York, resident Peter Obebeduo stole taxpayer checks totaling $89,000. The checks were made out to "I. R. S." (Internal Revenue Service) by three separate taxpayers. He was successful in cashing one of the three altered checks.

When he tried to cash the other two checks at a Livingston, New Jersey, bank, an alert bank teller spotted the alterations. The teller noticed that *I. R. S.* had been changed to *Iurus Products* and *Idris F. Mohammed.*

Obebeduo pleaded guilty to the possession of a forged financial document. He was sentenced to fifteen months in prison and ordered to repay $7,200—the amount of the successfully cashed check.

P R O J E C T :
The Case of the Possible Misprint

What You Need:
- **Figure 21**
- **clear metric ruler**

As a junior document examiner, you have been asked to examine a lottery ticket. Its owner stands to win over $2,000 if you can validate it.

The winning letter combination for the lottery is *O C M*. When the ticket in Figure 21a was put into a computer scanner, it was recorded as *D C M* and was not identified as the winning ticket. Figures 21b and 21c show known examples (standards) of *O* and *D* from other lottery tickets.

FIGURE 21

Evidence—The Case of the Possible Misprint

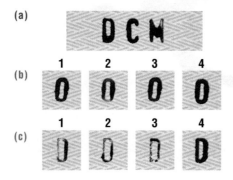

(a) Questioned lottery ticket.

(b) Lottery print standards for the letter "O."

(c) Lottery print standards for the letter "D."

What You Do:

1. Copy Table 7 into your notebook.
2. Examine each of the identically magnified machine-printed letter standards *O* and *D* from other lottery tickets in Figures 21b and 21c. Use a clear metric ruler to measure the width of each letter in millimeters (mm). Record these values in your data table.
3. Measure the first (left) letter in the questioned lottery ticket. Record its width, in millimeters, in the data table.
4. Based upon your measurement data, write an opinion for the court as to whether the lottery ticket in Figure 21a is a winning lottery ticket. Confirm your findings in Chapter 5.

TABLE 7. Letter Widths Data

	Letter 1 Size (mm)	Letter 2 Size (mm)	Letter 3 Size (mm)	Letter 4 Size (mm)
Lottery ticket standard for letter "O"				
Lottery ticket standard for letter "D"				
Questioned lottery ticket				

Science Project Idea

Using a computer with a word processing program, type a sentence having capitals, lowercase letters, and numerals. Copy and paste this original text nine times. Use the word processing program to make the following changes to each text line: (1) Add a number (1 through 10) to the beginning of the text line. (2) Change each of the text lines to a different 12-point font: (1) Arial, (2) Bookman Old Style, (3) Courier, (4) Copperplate Gothic Bold, (5) Engravers MT, (6) Garamond, (7) Palatino, (8) Symbol, (9) Times New Roman, and (10) Verdana.

Use a magnifying glass and a ruler to measure and compare letter height, width, and spacing. Make a table comparing these values for each font type.

Make copies of your data table and pass them around to your friends. Can they identify a particular font based upon your information?

The Case of the Wizard and His Pen

OBJECTIVE: To practice handwriting analysis

THE SCOUNDREL: Robert Spring (1813–1876)

THE CRIME: A significant forger in the United States was Robert Spring. He was a Philadelphia rare book dealer who used his business as a front for his criminal activity. He is best remembered for his many forgeries of George Washington. Spring's most common forgeries were of Revolutionary War passes—issued by the hand of George Washington.

Although Spring usually resorted to tracing, most of his Washington forgeries were done freehand—closely imitating Washington's flowing script. He was an unusual forger and marketing man—he would have a forgery, and a note asking for a sale, delivered to well-to-do individuals. In the note Spring would ask for money for the autographed letter. Usually he received it.

On November 4, 1869, Spring was arrested at his home in Philadelphia by Detective Franklin. Spring confessed his guilt when he was arrested. His forgery methods were outlined during his trial in 1869: "He would obtain, by some means, a genuine letter and then trace it on a sheet of paper, which he stained with coffee grounds to give it the appearance of age."

In and out of prison for the rest of his life, Spring died on December 14, 1876—seventy-seven years to the day after the death of his most-forged celebrity, George Washington.

PROJECT:
Handwriting Analysis

What You Need:

- pen
- pencil
- 7 sheets of white, unlined paper
- newspaper or book
- friends

What You Do:

1. Have a friend select another person who will be willing to prepare writing samples.

2. The writer needs to create a group of known examples of his or her writing. Your friend should have the writer draft one or two paragraphs, in cursive, on five clean sheets of paper using a pen. The writer should find paragraphs from a newspaper or a book to copy. Each writing sample should have a different text. Make sure that capital letters and numerals are used in each document. Tell your friend to label, in pencil, each of these five documents K-1 to K-5 (for known writing samples).

3. Tell your friend to select a single paragraph of text that has capitals and numerals. Have the writer copy

this single paragraph onto a clean sheet of paper in cursive to create a sixth document. Your friend should make a special mark in pencil, known only to him, that this document is the genuine one.

4. Tell your friend to select another writer who will be asked to try to *exactly imitate* the sixth document. Your friend should tell the writer to take as much care as possible in executing this forgery. Remind them that practice may make perfect! Your friend should make another special mark in pencil, known only to him, that identifies this document as the "forgery." In pencil, your friend should then label the sixth and seventh documents Q-1 and Q-2 (for "questioned" documents).

5. Have your friend deliver all seven documents for you to examine:
   - K-1 through K-5
   - Q-1 and Q-2

6. Follow the handwriting analysis steps (Chapter 2) when examining each of the seven documents. Make a document analysis table in your notebook. Can you determine which of the two questioned documents is genuine and which is the "forgery"?

Science Project Idea

Obtain handwritten document examples (five or more) from three or four people. Use the handwriting analysis technique to prepare a comparison analysis for each individual. Have one or two of these individuals give a friend additional handwritten documents. Ask your friend to mark each of these documents with an owner-ship mark. Can you identify the authors of the submitted writing samples?

●●●●●●●●●●●●●●●●●●●●●●●●●

The Case of the Questioned Page

OBJECTIVE: To analyze pencil markings

POE SCHOLAR: Dr. Burton R. Pollin

THE CRIME: "Buyer beware" is the watchword in buying historical documents or books with inscriptions. Unscrupulous dealers knowingly sell documents without detailed analysis or a documented history. Sometimes, even large auction houses are not careful in researching items they offer.

On January 3, 1995, a rare literary find of Edgar Allan Poe's was reported. A *New York Times* article spoke

of the discovery of eight lines of verse on a blank page of his first edition of *Tales of the Grotesque and Arabesque*, published in 1839. This particular book also had an inked inscription to Poe's cousin, Emily Virginia Chapman. The existence of such a unique

Edgar Allan Poe

article by Poe's hand was certainly news. It was a very valuable property—but was it genuine?

Since 1995, this book has been resold by a number of dealers, including Sotheby's and Christie's. In a Letter to the Editor, Dr. Burton R. Pollin, the editor of *Poe's Collected Writings*, writes, "The faint pencil markings had also escaped the close examination of experts." He continues, "Slim are the chances of Poe's writing such poor verses, and in pencil . . . on a different page from his (genuine) inked inscription." Dr. Pollin hopes the current owner would allow a closer inspection of the questioned page. He is concerned that the page is "the ilk of the numerous forgeries of Poe's handwriting created by one Joseph Cosey."

Many individuals, like Poe, rarely wrote in pencil, except to make corrections of their manuscripts. Both Joseph Cosey and Mark Hofmann were known for forging verse in pencil. But why forge a signed presentation copy—valuable in its own right? Allowing careful study may point the finger at one of them. Unfortunately, the current owner has not yet allowed independent examination of the document.

PROJECT:
Identifying Pencil Markings

What You Need:

- white index cards, unlined
- pencils having as many hardness values as you can find; both sharp and dull point

- **magnifying glass**
- **ballpoint pen**
- **sheet of paper**
- **2 friends**

The wooden pencil was invented in England in 1564. The first mass-produced pencils were made in Germany in 1662. Since 1795, powdered graphite, clay, water, and wax have been mixed and shaped into small-diameter rods called leads. These thin rods are then dried, and heated to very high temperatures. Changing the amount of clay and baking time determines the degree of hardness of the lead.

In the early nineteenth century, English pencil makers began using a letter designation for varying hardness. The letter indicated the graphite-to-clay ratio. Softer leads were designated with B (for *black*: more graphite), harder leads with H (for *hard*: more clay). The hardest is a 9H, followed by 8H, 7H, 6H, 5H, 4H, 3H, 2H, and H. F is the middle of the hardness scale; then comes HB, B, 2B, 3B, 4B, 5B, 6B, 7B, 8B, and 9B, which is the softest. Another grading method uses numbers; the equivalents would be #1 = B, #2 = HB, #2½ = F, #3 = H, and #4 = 2H.

Colored pencils are pencils whose marking pigment is not black. Special blue copy pencils have a dye that will not appear if the document is photocopied. Some red pencil markings will glow under UV light.

What You Do:

Make a reference collection of pencil markings. You will use this collection as a guide in comparing pencil markings. Collect examples of as many hardness values as you can find. Figure 22 has examples of many common pencil hardnesses. Use unlined white index cards for your collection. Write the type (No. and letter) at the top of the card with a ballpoint pen. Then write (for example) "No. 2—HB pencil; sharp point" on the card with the corresponding pencil.

A dull point will make a wide mark (or stroke). The amount of downward pressure when writing will make a depression on the paper—like that of a toboggan on snow. Different people write using different downward pressure. The softer the lead, the darker the marking. (See Figure 22.)

1. From your collection of pencils, select four: two of the same hardness type, sharp point and dull point.
2. With a ballpoint pen, number four new index cards 1 through 4.
3. Have two friends each take two cards and two pencils. Have them write an identical message (e.g., "The game is afoot") on each card using a different pencil. Suggest that one friend press down while writing. Have your friends keep track of card number, pencil type, point size, and pressure used.
4. Tell your friends to record the following on a separate sheet of paper:

FIGURE 22

Guide to Pencil Markings

(a)

6H 4H 2H

(b)

8B 4B HB

(c)

soft lead; dull point medium lead; dull point hard lead; dull point

(d)

Magnified (10X) views of hard and soft lead pencil markings.

(a) hard leads: 6H, 4H, 2H; (b) soft leads: 8B, 4B, HB; (c) dull point; (d) orange pencil

- the card number(s) they wrote on
- the pencil hardness type used for each card number
- the point characteristic (sharp or dull) for each card number

5. Use a magnifying glass to examine each numbered index card. Based on your reference collection of pencil markings, determine what pencil type (hardness), point characteristic (sharp or dull), and pressure level was used to make each pencil marking. Can you tell which friend pressed down while writing? See Chapter 5 for a sample analysis.

Science Project Idea

Some colored pencil markings cannot be photocopied. Visit an art supply store. Purchase a copy pencil along with other colored pencils. Write the color and manufacturer's name of each pencil on a clean sheet of white paper. Photocopy the page. Which type(s) did not photocopy?

Try blending various pencil colors to create a color that will not photocopy. Can you do it?

CHAPTER 4

Investigating the Crime

This chapter introduces a "crime" that you and your friends can solve using the information and skills you learned in this book. Based upon an actual historical profile, you will create documents for examination. One document will be "genuine." It will have a known paper type, size, watermark, ink, and pen from a known period, and be written in a known hand. Other documents will be forgeries— missing genuine features. Your friends' job will be to identify the genuine document and expose the fakes. They should be able to support their "expert opinions" by assembling "findings of fact" in a report to you.

THE PROFILE:

The Case of the Hudson Doggerel

Edgar Allan Poe (1809–1849) was the only major American writer to attend the U.S. Military Academy at West Point (1830–1831). Poe wrote poems for his cadet audience there. He was noted for his many comic verses. Very few of these lines of wit survive. One surviving poem was written to honor Lieutenant Joseph Locke, who taught military tactics. Locke was also the inspector, responsible for reporting all infractions of the rules. Poe usually sent his manuscripts to Elam Bliss, his publisher on Hudson Street in New York. It was Poe's habit to use initials instead of full names when addressing his letters.

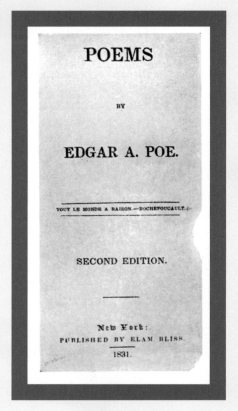

Poe preferred to use special light gray paper sheets for his verses. This was a fine, unlined, quarto paper with laid lines and a large watermark. He had a supply at the academy, purchased from a New York merchant. He mostly used a steel-nibbed pen, and was fond of iron-gall (brown) ink. Sometimes he did make pencil notations or corrections—crossing out words and rewriting in pencil. Poe had a peculiar habit of using colored pencils to write dedications. He was methodical in folding his paper sheets into thirds, and he usually addressed the folded top flap.

What You Need:

- ["GENUINE"] sheet (8½ x 11") Southworth® Private Stock light gray laid paper (at office supply store)
- ["GENUINE"] brown fountain pen ink (Waterman's® brand)
- ["GENUINE"] steel-nibbed pen (fountain pen)
- ["GENUINE"] red pencil

- [FORGERY 1] sheet (8½ x 11") gray copier paper
- [FORGERY 1] rollerball pen using brown gel ink
- [FORGERY 1] ruler
- [FORGERY 2] sheet (4 x 6") blue-lined notepaper
- 5 index cards
- No. 2 (HB) pencil
- ink eraser
- magnifying glass
- black light (UV light source)
- desk lamp
- scissors
- paper cutter
- pencil reference collection (see Case #10)
- chromatography setup (see Case #2)
- yourself acting as Edgar Allan Poe
- 2 friends acting as forgers
- a friend, or friends, acting as the document examiner(s)
- an adult

What You Do:

1. Use brown fountain pen ink (Waterman's® brand) and a fountain pen. In cursive, in your hand, make five copies of the following text, on five index cards, that will become known writing standards. Poe wrote this text to his publisher, Elam Bliss, in 1831.

    A poem, in my opinion, is opposed to a work of science by having, for its immediate object, pleasure, and not truth.

2. Create the "GENUINE" document:
    a. **Under adult supervision**, use a paper cutter to professionally trim the 8½ x 11-inch

Southworth® light gray laid paper sheet to a final dimension of 8 x 10 inches—the quarto size used by Poe.

b. Write the text (using the same fountain pen with Waterman's® brown ink) in your hand on the cut Southworth® light gray 8 x 10-inch laid paper:

(center of page, ink)

John Locke was a notable name;
Joe Locke is a greater; in short,
The former was well known to fame,
But the latter's well known "to report."

c. Fold the document in thirds.

d. Write, in your hand, the following note:

(top fold, red pencil)

Letter to—B

3. Create the FORGERY 1 document:

a. Have FORGER 1 study the five written index cards to attempt to master your handwriting style. Encourage your "forger" to practice your handwriting.

b. Using a ruler, measure ½ inch from the top of the 8½ x 11-inch sheet of gray copy paper and draw a cut line using a No. 2 (HB) pencil.

c. Using a ruler, measure 1 inch from the side of the 8½ x 11-inch sheet of copy paper and draw a cut line using a No. 2 pencil.

d. Use scissors to cut the sheet to a final size of 8 x 10 inches.

e. Have FORGER 1 imitate your handwriting to create the document text using a brown gel ink pen:

(center of page, ink)

John Locke was a notable person;
Joe Locke is a greater; in short,
The former was well known to fame,
But the latter's well known "to report."

f. Use a No. 2 HB pencil to cross out *person* and write *name* above it.

g. Have FORGER 1 fold the paper into thirds.

h. Have FORGER 1 write the following note:

(top fold—red pencil)

Letter to—Mr. Elam Bliss

4. Create the FORGERY 2 document:

a. Have FORGER 2 study the five written index cards to master your handwriting style. Encourage your "forger" to practice your handwriting.

b. Have FORGER 2 imitate your handwriting to create the document text on blue-lined paper using a No. 2 (HB) pencil:

(center of page—No. 2 pencil)

John Locke was a notable name;
Joe Locke is a greater; in short,
The former was well known to fame,
But the latter's well known "to report."

c. Have FORGER 2 use an ink eraser and erase *to report* and rewrite it using the same pencil.

102

    d. Have FORGER 2 fold the paper into thirds.

    e. Have FORGER 2 write the following note:

(top fold, red pencil)

To—E. B.
35 Pearl Street
New York

5. Photocopy the "Profile" on pages 98–99 and give it to your DOCUMENT EXAMINER. The profile provides basic historical information about the "author" of the document. The document examiner should have the following analysis materials: magnifying glass, desk lamp, black light, pencil reference collection, and chromatography setup.

6. Have the DOCUMENT EXAMINER perform an analysis of all three documents to determine which is the "GENUINE" document. The analysis should include a "findings of fact" report.

7. Compare the DOCUMENT EXAMINER's findings to those in Chapter 5.

Project Analyses

This chapter contains the analysis findings for each of the cases presented in this book.

CHAPTER 2
Practicing Your Paper Analysis Skills

Sheet #1 is watercolor paper:
- Size 8 ½ x 11 inches is commercially available.
- Sheet is very thick.
- UV examination shows no brighteners.
- Fountain pen ink bleeds; no coating applied.
- Watermark is visible in transmitted light.
- Fiber content is cotton; no wood fiber.

Sheet #2 is modern fine writing paper:
- Size 8 ½ x 11 inches is commercially available.
- Sheet is thin, 20-pound weight.
- UV examination shows optical brighteners. Sheet is "modern," made after 1970.
- Fountain pen ink does not bleed; coating applied.
- Watermark is visible in transmitted light.
- Fiber content is cotton; no wood fiber.

Sheet #3 is modern copier paper:
- Size 8 ½ x 11 inches is commercially available.
- Sheet is thin, 20-pound weight.

- UV examination shows optical brighteners. Sheet is "modern," made after 1970.
- Fountain pen ink does not bleed; coating applied.
- No watermark is visible in transmitted light.
- Fiber content is cotton and wood fiber.

Sheet #4 has been forged to appear as correspondence paper used in 1889.

- Size 4 x 5 inches was common in the late 1800s.
- Sheet has been stained to give the appearance of age.
- Sheet has markings (tiny holes or other markings) indicating that it was hung to dry.
- UV examination shows optical brighteners. Sheet is "modern," made after 1970.
- Fountain pen ink bleeds; coating has washed away.
- No watermark is visible in transmitted light.
- Fiber content is cotton and wood fiber.

Sheet #5 is simulated correspondence paper used in 1824.

- Size 8 x 10 inches was common in the early 1800s.
- UV examination shows no optical brighteners.
- Fountain pen ink does not bleed; paper had coating.
- Watermark and laid lines are visible in transmitted light.
- Fiber content is cotton.

●●●●●●●●●●●●●●●●

CHAPTER 3

CASE #1. The Case of the President's Signatur

FIGURE 23. Case #1 Analysis

(a)

(b)

(c)

(d)

(a) Martin Van Buren (forgery). In President Van Buren's genuine signature, the letters M, V, and B are linked. The V also has a distinctive curlicue. This signature shows separate capital letters M and V. It is a forgery.

(b) Martin van Buren (genuine). Notice the connected M, V, and B, as well as the curlicue.

(c) Lori Miner (genuine). The arrow points out the unique style when she writes the "o" in Lori. The dashed line shows the slope of the letter M.

(d) Lori Miner (forgery). Notice the lack of unique "o" signing style as well as the different slant of the letter M.

CASE #2. The Case of the Deadly Message Label

FIGURE 24. *Case #2 Analysis*

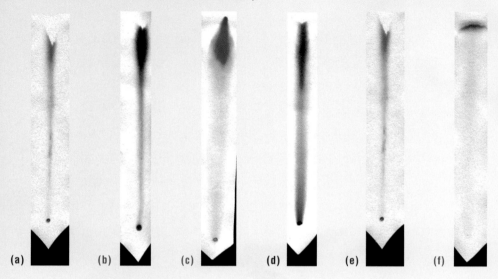

(a) (b) (c) (d) (e) (f)

(a) Uniball®—blue ink (blue)
(b) Uniball®—black ink (black)
(c) Pilot®—blue ink (dark blue, purple, light blue)
(d) Pilot®—black ink (black)
(e) Sheaffer® fountain pen (blue)
(f) Sheaffer® fountain pen—black ink (green, purple, blue)

CASE #3. The Case of the Implicating Impression

Figure 25 analyzes the two techniques. Both methods—side lighting and graphite rubbing—are equally effective as shown. However, the graphite method is not used because it cannot be undone; once the graphite is applied, it cannot be removed without compromising or changing the quality of the evidence. Examining the paper surface with side lighting shows some writing indentations that can be studied—without damaging the evidence.

Today, a far more sensitive technique is used. ESDA, the electrostatic detection apparatus, can reveal paper indentations many sheets below the original writing sample. The paper sheet is placed on the device and is covered by a plastic sheet. The unit is turned on and the paper receives an electrostatic charge. A mixture of copier toner and tiny glass beads is poured over the protective plastic sheet. The indentations on the paper attract the toner, and the paper marks are interpreted.

FIGURE 25. Case #3 Analysis

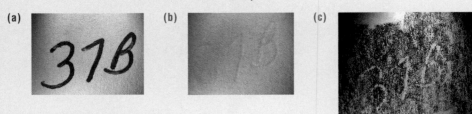

(a)   Original ballpoint pen ink line, 37B.

(b)   10X magnified side-lighted image of the underlying sheet; "37B" is revealed.

(c)   Graphite rubbing of the underlying sheet.

CASE #4. The Case of the Signature That Was Not Real

Only (b) is a hand signature (see Figure 26). The other two signatures are stamped. The hand signature is in blue ballpoint ink. Notice the flowing patches of light and dark areas of the ink line. Also notice that there is a darkened area wherever two ink lines cross each other. The stamped signatures (a and c) have some telltale line characteristics:

- The ink line is evenly blue, with no light areas.
- There are no dark patches where ink lines cross.
- There are tiny line breaks in (c).

FIGURE 26. *Case #4 Analysis*

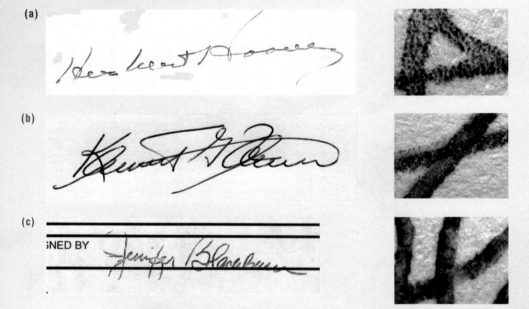

(a)

(b)

(c)

SNED BY

Both Clinton signatures are autopens. Copies on clear acetate sheet match exactly. No signature (unless it is a facsimile copy) is exactly like another.

CASE #5. The Case of the Windsor Note

TABLE 6. Data for UV & White Light Examination of Documents

	COLOR (room light)	COLOR (UV light)
Paper sample 1a	white	glows purple
Paper sample 1b	white	Center UV "dull"
Paper sample 2a	white	glows purple
Paper sample 2b	white	center of sheet UV "dull"
Paper sample 3a	white	glows purple
Paper sample 3b	white	center of sheet UV "dull"
Paper sample 4a	gray	does not glow
Paper sample 4b	gray	no UV "dull" area
Ink sample 1a	orange	ink glows
Ink sample 1b	orange faded	ink glows
Ink sample 2a	blue	No glow
Ink sample 2b	blue completely faded	No glow
Ink sample 3a	yellow	intense yellow glow
Ink sample 3b	yellow faded	intense yellow glow
Ink sample 4a	pink	faint pink glow
Ink sample 4b	pink faded	faint pink glow

Step 5:

- Most premium copier papers have optical brighteners.
- Fine writing papers, depending on the manufacturer, may have brighteners added.
- The paper industry uses a 100-point scale; most optical brighteners are advertised at 60 "brightness value" points. The glow and color intensity will be greater for higher brightness values.
- Clear acrylic will change the appearance of the paper under UV light.

Step 10:

- Some ink dyes are soluble in water and wash out. Most fluorescent dyes are not soluble in water and remain. Most fluorescent dyes are invisible in white (e.g. room) light. Since the fluorescent dyes are not washed out, they can be seen under UV light but are invisible in white light.
- Some inks contain pigments that can be dissolved in water. If a document written with these inks is submerged in water, these water-soluble inks will be dissolved and washed away. If no other water insoluble inks are present, then the ink line will disappear.
- Inks that cannot be dissolved in water are called insoluble. If a document written with an insoluble ink (e.g. a permanent ink) is immersed in water, the ink will not be washed away.

FIGURE 27.   *Case #5 Analysis*

(a)
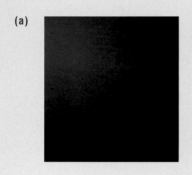

(b)

(c)
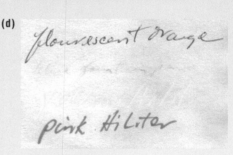

(d)
flourescent orange
blue fountain pen
yellow HiLiter
pink Hi Liter

(a) Paper with optical brighteners appear deep purple under UV light.

(b) The circled area of the paper was treated with clear acrylic, which blocks UV light; the paper appears lighter.

(c) Inks before water submersion.

(d) Inks after water submersion.

(e) Inks under UV light after water submersion.

(e)
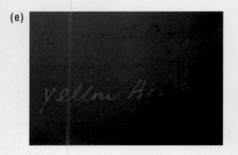

- Some inks contain chemicals that glow when exposed to wavelengths of light shorter than violet light—ultraviolet light. In white light, the same ink containing the fluorescent colorant does not glow.

- Inks containing water-soluble colorants would show banding patterns if a chromatogram was made of them. Any non water-soluble component (e.g. a fluorescent colorant) would remain in or very close to the original ink spot. If the paper strip was exposed to UV light, the application spot would appear to glow while the other color bands would become invisible.

Some papermakers use optical brighteners (OBs) to make their paper look bright and white. Under UV light, these OBs make the paper glow purple (Figure 27a). Paper without OBs will look gray under UV light. Banknote paper does not contain OBs. To achieve this UV dulling effect, some counterfeiters will apply a clear acrylic to paper so that it will appear UV dull (Figure 27b).

CASE #6. The Case of the Questioned Photocopy

Figure 28 illustrates a possible result from this case. Of course, your results may vary.

Document Analysis:

1. The complimentary close, with genuine signature, was overcopied onto the body of another document.
2. Both the body and complimentary close of the composite document used Courier 12-point typeface. This composite document is

a first generation photocopy, as there are very few, if any, stray markings or individual letter character deterioration. If there were more stray markings or more variation in typeface sizes, it would be a sign that numerous photocopies had been made.

FIGURE 28. *Case #6 Analysis*

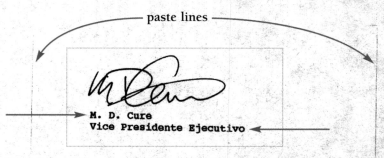

November 6, 1969

COMMUNICACION CONFIDENOIAL

Señor J.C. Lesley,
Guatemala, Guatemala, C.A.

Señor J.C. Lesley,

Sirvano tomar nota de las siguientes instrucio nes acordadas por las oficinas centrals de Jersey City, N.J.

En resuumeni el monto de los honorarios del Lic. Palacies en al Juicio referido que qun no la han side cancel dos, seran fijados por el Tribunal, por acuerdo expreso con 81.
Al notificarle a Ud. Como representanta de la Emtar el monie que arraja tal liquidqcion.

——— paste lines ———

M. D. Cure
Vice Presidente Ejecutivo

CASE #8. The Case of the Misdirected Tax Payment

TABLE 7. Letter Widths Data

	LETTER 1 SIZE (mm)	LETTER 2 SIZE (mm)	LETTER 3 SIZE (mm)	LETTER 4 SIZE (mm)
Lottery ticket standard for letter "O"	4	4	4	4
Lottery ticket for letter "D"	3	3	3	3.5
Questioned lottery ticket	3.5			

The width of the questioned letter is under 4 mm wide, which is below all the standard measurements for the letter "O" and within the standard for the letter "D." Therefore the first letter of the questioned lottery ticket is a "D."

CASE #10. The Case of the Questioned Page

In this example, the following pencil types were selected:

CARD #1: 2B (sharp point)

CARD #2: 3H (sharp point)

CARD #3: 2B (dull point)

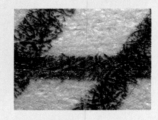

CARD #4: 3H (dull point)

Four pencils were selected: soft (2B) and hard (3H) pencil leads; each lead type had a dull point and a sharp point.

●●●●●●●●●●●●●●●●

CHAPTER 4

The Case of the Hudson Doggerel

Findings:

1. The document addressed to publisher Elam Bliss ("Letter to—B") in red pencil is the "GENUINE" document:

Findings of fact:

- Poe used pearl-gray paper while in New York.
- The contemporary Southworth® gray paper contains laid lines and a watermark, just like GENUINE Poe documents of 1830 onward.
- Poe used iron-gall ink (simulated by the Waterman's® brown fountain pen ink).
- Poe did send correspondence to his publisher, Elam Bliss, addressing it as "Letter to—B"
- The quarto (8 x 10 inches) was the sheet size used by Poe.
- The paper has a definite watermark, "SOUTH-WORTH® Private Stock."
- The paper may not be modern (ca. 1970s or later)—it contains no optical brighteners (it does not glow purple under UV light).
- The handwriting in the document agrees with the five known standards used for comparison based upon a handwriting analysis comparing the document with five known writing samples (on white index cards).

2. The document addressed "Letter to—Mr. Elam Bliss" is a forgery.

Findings of fact:

- Although the paper is gray, it contains no laid lines or watermark under examination using transmitted light. They are not visible when the sheet is held up to a window or lightbulb.
- The folded document shows marks of being cut. Pencil markings are also observed. (Many forgers would cut pages from books of a known time period to get genuine period paper.)
- The paper is modern grey; it has added optical brighteners (it glows purple under UV light).
- The handwriting in the document does not agree with the five known standards (on white index cards). This is based upon a handwriting analysis done comparing the writing in the document with the five known examples.
- The folded paper shows a crossed-out mistake. While Poe did use pencil to correct a manuscript, he would have written out an error-free copy for his publisher.
- Although Poe would have used a red editor's pencil to write a note, he would have never addressed his publisher correspondence to "Mr." He rarely used Bliss's full name.

3. The fully addressed document is a crude forgery.

Findings of fact:

- The paper is modern, of the wrong size (not quarto), and is lined.
- Poe never used lined paper.
- The paper shows signs of erasure (fourth line, "to report"). Poe always crossed out mistakes.
- The note in red pencil is a complete fabrication— Elam Bliss's place of business was on Hudson Street, not Pearl Street, in New York. Poe never placed an address on a manuscript for publication.
- The handwriting in the document does not agree with the five known standards (on white index cards). This is based upon a handwriting analysis done comparing the writing in the document with the five known examples.

GLOSSARY

altered document—A document that contains some change, either an addition or deletion.

autopen—A mechanical device that is used to create a signature pattern.

ballpoint pen—A writing instrument having a small, freely rotating ball as its writing tip. The ball rolls non-water-based ink onto paper.

chromatography—A chemistry technique used to separate a mixture of dissolved colored materials such as dyes on a porous material such as paper. The result is a paper strip called a chromatogram.

colorant—A colored substance; either a dye or a pigment added to ink.

colored pencil—Pencil whose marking pigment is not black.

cursive—Writing in which letters in each word are joined together.

direct copy—The first photocopy made of an original document.

direct lighting—Light that shines from a source evenly onto an object.

disguised writing—Writing that is deliberately altered in order to hide the writer's identity.

document—Material, such as paper, containing marks, symbols, or signs that convey a message. Many documents are written by ink, pencil, or machine on paper.

document examiner—An individual who scientifically studies the details of documents.

dye—A colored substance that dissolves completely in a liquid. It gives color to an ink.

erasure—The removal or evidence of removal of writing, typewriting, or printing from a document by physical or chemical means.

evidence—Any testimony, documents, or material objects presented at a trial to prove the existence or nonexistence of a fact.

expert witness—An individual who has special training or experience that is permitted to state an opinion in court regarding a matter in question.

fiber—A thread.

findings—Legal conclusions acceptable by the court.

fluorescence—A property of a material to give off light under special circumstances (e.g., under ultraviolet light).

flowback—The accumulation of ink at the end of a line made by a pen nib when it is lifted from the paper.

forensic science—The field of science used in the judicial process.

forgery—A non-genuine document or signature.

fountain pen—A writing instrument containing a reservoir of ink and having a nib as the writing tip.

fraud—Intentional deceit.

fraudulent (forged) signature—The signing of someone else's name, done without permission and often with some amount of imitation.

graphite—A form of carbon used in pencils.

habit—A repeated detail that may serve to individualize handwriting.

hand lettering—A style of writing in which each letter is written separately.

handwriting analysis expert—A document examiner.

hesitation stroke—Irregular, jerky, or shaky line of writing.

known document—A document that can be proven genuine.

laid line—Closely placed lines visible under transmitted light in handmade papers, resulting from the wires used to string the wooden frame in which the paper was molded.

line mark (stroke)—A mark made by a pencil, pen, or other writing instrument.

magnification—How much an object is made larger than when viewed by the naked eye.

mark—A visible written symbol.

microscopic examination—A study made using a magnifying glass or microscope.

Mormon Church—The Church of Jesus Christ of Latter-day Saints, the largest denomination within the Latter-day Saint movement (Mormonism). The Church was founded by Joseph Smith in 1830, with headquarters in Salt Lake City, Utah.

nib—The pointed part of a writing instrument that distributes ink.

oblique (side-angle) light—Light that is controlled to strike the surface of a document from one side at a very low angle.

obliteration—The covering over of marks or writing in a document to hide them.

optical brighteners—Chemical(s) used to increase the apparent whiteness of paper. The chemical substance reflects ultraviolet light, thus increasing the amount of visible light reflected. Papers containing optical brighteners will appear purple under fluorescent light.

original document—A created document; not a copy.

overcopy—To place a document over another and photocopy both to produce a new overcopied or combined document.

overwriting (insertion)—Changing a document by adding (inserting) a letter, word, or sentence to a document by someone other than the author. Usually these marks can be identified by a difference in writing material or differences in handwriting.

pen—Any writing instrument used to apply inks.

pencil—A writing instrument in which the marking portion is a stick of compressed graphite or colored marking substance usually mixed with clays and waxes.

pen lift—An interruption of a stroke caused by removing the pen from the paper.

pigment—Colored material that does not dissolve in a liquid. It gives color to an ink.

pretrial report—A summary of the facts of a case including conclusions based on analysis.

provenance—Proof of a document's authenticity or of past ownership.

quality—A distinct characteristic. In handwriting, "quality" is used to describe an identifying character related to the writing movement itself.

questioned document—A document under review because of unknown or argued facts.

rag paper—Paper made from 100 percent cotton fibers; usually from discarded cotton rag material.

rollerball pen—A type of ballpoint pen that distributes water-based inks onto paper.

sample—A selected part used to represent the whole.

signature—A person's name, written in a distinctive manner; a legal form of identification or authorization.

sizing—A treatment used on paper that gives it a surface finish that is resistant to the penetration of inks or other liquids.

soluble—Able to be dissolved (usually in water).

stamped signature—An authorized form of a signature that can be mechanically applied to a document.

standard—A genuine example. Used by the document examiner as the basis for comparison to a questioned document.

testimony—Evidence given by a knowledgeable witness, under oath, as compared to evidence from writings and other sources.

traced forgery—A document made by following the outline of a genuine line with a writing instrument.

transmitted light—Light that shines through an object.

tremor—A writing weakness illustrated by irregular, shaky strokes.

type—Printed characters or letters.

typeface—A particular design of type.

ultraviolet (UV) light (black light)—Light having a wavelength shorter than visible violet light.

vehicle—The liquid part of an ink.

watermark—Translucent design impressed in certain papers during their manufacture.

white light—Light having all visible colors: red, orange, yellow, green, blue, indigo, and violet.

writing impression (indentation)—Writing marks without pigment made on paper in a tablet or stack immediately below that which received a visible writing mark.

FURTHER READING

BOOKS

Camenson, Blythe. *Opportunities in Forensic Science Careers.* Chicago: VGM Career Books, 2001.

Conklin, Barbara Gardner, Robert Gardner, and Dennis Shortelle. *Encyclopedia of Forensic Science: A Compendium of Detective Fact and Fiction.* Westport, Conn.: Oryx Press, 2002.

Fridell, Ron. *Solving Crimes: Pioneers of Forensic Science.* New York: Franklin Watts, 2000.

Morgan, Marilyn. *Careers in Criminology.* New York: McGraw-Hill, 2000.

Owen, David. *Police Lab: How Forensic Science Tracks Down and Convicts Criminals.* Buffalo, N.Y.: Firefly Books Ltd., 2002.

Platt, Richard. *Crime Scene: The Ultimate Guide to Forensic Science.* London: Dorling Kindersley, Ltd., 2003.

Rainis, Kenneth G. *Crime-Solving Science Projects: Forensic Science Experiments.* Berkeley Heights, N.J.: Enslow Publishers, Inc., 2000.

Ramsland, Katherine. *The Forensic Science of C.S.I.* San Francisco: Berkley Publishing Group, 2001.

INTERNET ADDRESSES

American Society of Questioned Document Examiners.
 <http://www.asqde.org>

CourtTV.com. *Forensics in the Classroom.* © 2002.
 <http://www.courttv.com/forensics%5Fcurriculum/>

Federal Bureau of Investigation. *FBI Youth.*
 <http://www.fbi.gov/kids/6th12th/6th12th.htm>

INDEX